Student
Entrepreneurs

Student Entrepreneurs

MENTORS MATTER

Author
MICHAEL McMYNE

Edited by
DENISE OTILLIO

Student Entrepreneurs: Mentors Matter
Michael McMyne
Executive Editor: Denise Otillio

First Edition 2009

Published by Smurfit-Stone Center for Entrepreneurship,
John Cook School of Business, Saint Louis University

Copyright © 2009 Saint Louis University

Designed by Todd Lape / Lape Designs

Printed in the United States of America.

ISBN 978-0-9777190-1-3

This book is dedicated to
MENTORS throughout the globe.
The unselfish actions you take
to mold our dreams will never be
forgotten and will always be cherished.

Contents

Foreword

BY VINCE IPPOLITO

"The only source of knowledge is experience"

—ALBERT EINSTEIN

Upon graduation from college, if someone would have asked me what did mentoring or being an entrepreneur mean to me, I would have had a simple answer, "Learning how to make pizza in my father's Italian restaurant." I grew up in an Italian family who owned and operated an Italian restaurant. One of those factors offered me enough stories that could easily provide the situations for a successful TV sitcom. The other factor provided me with the experiences and knowledge that an MBA program could never have offered to me. My father is my teacher, and the first lesson that I internalized from his experience seems obvious, but it is a lesson that is often missed or ignored: Success is a product of hard work. After the death of his own father, my father dropped out of high school in order to support his mother and sisters. From that point on, my father worked hard to build a successful family business, the restaurant. His hard work and an instinct for business equaled success. Although we did not realize it then, my family was entrepreneurs. Not only did we not realize our role as entrepreneurs, we did not understand fully what that role meant; we just enjoyed what we did. We also did not realize that we had mentors. Everyone who we could learn from became our mentors. Did we call them mentors? No. We simply called these invaluable people who help to direct our successful course, family and friends.

Unlike my father, I realized a couple of years after my college graduation that I was much better at ordering pizza from a menu than I was at making it in my family's restaurant. As a result, I decided to enter the corporate world as a sales representative. Less than one year later, that company downsized. Only two sales representatives were retained in that downsizing; I was one of them. I was told that one of the senior managers saw some potential in me. Because of this potential, I would remain his staff. I did not know then that this senior manager had chosen to mentor me. I did not know or refer to him as a mentor, I simply thought he was a nice guy. Initially, the sales division was struggling. Although my mentor spent as much time with me as he could, we both understood that neither I nor his role as mentor was first on his list of priorities. After several months of the business weakening, I was told when they had a project for me, they would give me a call. Otherwise, I was not to report to work. One week in this situation was all I could take. I decided to seek out some comfort food and counsel from my original mentor. In other words, I shared an anchovy pizza with my dad. Over that family meal, I wanted to see what he would do in my situation. His message was simple, and I have never forgotten it.

He said, "Create value in your company. Just because you're not working in the family business anymore, doesn't mean you're not an entrepreneur. Your company is struggling, which means they don't have all the answers. Help them find the answers, and you will create value for yourself. Never assume the guys on the top have all the answers; they got there by listening and learning from others. Find a solution to one of their problems and go fix it! If they don't have a job for you, create one and be the best at it. Now quit your complaining and eat your pizza." That advice and that moment defined the role of mentor: available, direct, passionate, simple, and compelling.

I listened, and I left to follow my father's advice. I believed in my value, and they believed. The company that was once failing is now one of the largest pharmaceutical companies in the world. The sales representative who was told to remain home became the Executive Vice President of Marketing and Sales.

As my career progressed, I continued to seek out mentors and to remain open and willing to listen. Without a doubt, without the help of my many mentors along the way, I could never have been as fortunate or given so many opportunities throughout my career. In essence, my success is a culmination of the people who have helped me. Among the many valuable lessons I have learned is that a young entrepreneur cannot be mentored if he doesn't know what areas need to be improved. I have seen many people more talented than I who were not open to a mentor's knowledge or wisdom. Consequently, their careers typically have had a short run. The importance of mentors and the wisdom that they give can never be downplayed.

The role of mentor may never appear on the resume of a successful businessman. It should. That role is probably one of the most important contributions to the climate of the business world that a successful entrepreneur can make. Why? Because it is the mentor's impression, tone, and vision that help to energize and inspire the drive and desire and dreams of a younger inventor, creator, director, leader. To paraphrase Albert Einstein, it is the experience of the mentor that becomes the source of knowledge of the young entrepreneur. An impressive company has mentored: Aristotle mentored Alexander the Great, Bach mentored Mozart, and, more recently, Eddy Merckx, the five-time Tour de France winner, mentored Lance Armstrong!

I am fortunate to be in that company. I was first introduced to the person who I would mentor, the author, Michael McMyne, when he interviewed with me for a sales position. I told him, "Mr. McMyne, we only hire people that could make a difference, our company is filled with talented people, and we are all driven to make this company a success." I went on to explain that we did not have jobs here, only opportunities, the entrepreneurial spirit, and a willingness to help others grow. If this is what he wanted, then Michael McMyne would succeed. He did want what the company espoused, and he did succeed. Michael went on to win our highest sales representative award in his first year, The Circle of Excellence, and graduated our leadership development program with flying colors in his second year. And now, this book is his fifth and final book in a series of success stories of globally recognized student entrepreneurs. In the process of compiling this unique book, Michael has taken the time to personally interview each of these students. During the course of the series, Michael founded McMyne & Associates, was named the Global Student Entrepreneur of the Year for Social Impact, and continues to be one of the top sales representatives in our company. I know that Michael has practiced what he is preaching, and he now wants to share this experience and wisdom with all of you. As his mentor, I applaud him. In a sense, that is the final pleasure of the mentor. He first recognizes the talent, then, directs it, cues it, critiques it, and finally, applauds the fine performance.

Finding people with a true entrepreneurial spirit inside them is a gift. Bringing it out in them is a joy. Sharing it with others is what makes you great.

Preface

BY PETER H. THOMAS

"A wise man learns from experience; a wiser man

learns from the experience of others."

—CHINESE PROVERB

In reading the accomplishments and insights of the talented young entrepreneurs featured in this book, I am inspired and impressed by their ingenuity and dedication in creating new, successful ventures. The underlying theme in these remarkable stories is the role that mentorship has played in the lives of these young entrepreneurs as they met the challenges of launching and developing their enterprises. I strongly believe that having mentors in your life is one of the key ingredients to achieving your goals; it certainly has been for me.

Throughout my life and business career as serial and social entrepreneur, I did not hesitate to surround myself with mentors in all the
areas I felt I needed guidance. I have found that there is a great deal
of inspiration and learning you can take away from the experiences
of your mentors. I have been privileged to have had the best mentors, and I attribute much of the success I have enjoyed to listening
to their caring and thoughtful advice. However, I've learned over
the years that for a mentor-mentee relationship to be successful, it
is crucial that the individuals we choose as mentors in our lives have
values that align with ours. Having that common ground or understanding to build a relationship from is essential.

Mentoring is one of the oldest forms of learning and it must
be so for a reason. According to Merriam-Webster, the term "mentor" dates back to Greek mythology when Odysseus, leaving for the
Trojan War, entrusts the education of his son Telemachus to his
friend Mentor. From this point forward, the word "mentor" became
synonymous with an individual who is an experienced and trusted
adviser, counselor, or guide.[1] Just like the many great leaders in history who surrounded themselves with trusted advisers, most of us
identify someone who has impacted our lives in a significant and
positive way. Such a person is usually older (but doesn't have to be if
they are an expert in the field) and always more experienced in the

---

1. Oxford Dictionary

particular area we seek advice, thus able to become our role model, challenger, and guide.[2] According to Shea[3], "mentoring is one of the broadest methods of encouraging human growth [...] where "one person invests time, energy, and personal know-how assisting the growth and ability of another person." Given these thoughts, mentors truly can be a pipeline of knowledge; we just have to learn to plug into it.

Mentors can be real or virtual. If you really study a person, you can tap into his or her knowledge even if you aren't about to communicate with him or her directly. When I started my first company, my lawyer told me that I needed to appoint some directors who could give the company wisdom, direction, and advice on strategy among others. I was 28 years old and had not met enough people at that time that I felt could give me the advice that I would need. I kept trying to think of people who could help me in this growth stage of my life. One day I was flipping though the pages of a beautiful book of black and white photographs by Yousaf Karsch. Among the portraits were those of John F. Kennedy, Martin Luther King, Mohandas Gandhi, and Ernest Hemingway. A thought occurred to me that these individuals could become my directors or my virtual boardroom in

---

2. Thomas, P. (2005). *LifeManual: A Proven Formula to Create the Life You Desire*. LifePilot Publication.

3. Shea, G. (2001). *Mentoring : How to develop successful mentor behaviors*. Menlo Park, CA: Course Technology Crisp.

a sense. I read everything about them that I could get my hands on and decided that given their wisdom and experience, they could advise me on what to do. So I cut their pictures out of the book, framed them and hung them in my office. As challenges came into my life, I would ask each one of them what they would do about the particular situation at hand. I found that JFK was the business advisor and Martin Luther King was the person who could tell me what was right and what was wrong as he was a great decision maker. Gandhi was my spiritual guide and Hemingway was the rouge to help me lighten up a bit when things got tense. If I needed an excuse to have a little fun, I would be sure to ask Ernest!

Virtual mentorship gives us the opportunity to access the wisdom of the ages as a valuable complement to current knowledge and best practices. Whether from the past or the present, we choose trusted advisors and role models not only for what they know or have done, but for what they stand for and how they resonate with our own values.

The world's most admired leaders have one distinct quality in common: "strong beliefs about matters of principle" or in other words, "they all have, or had, unwavering commitment to a clear set of values."⁴ For the past forty years, I have led my life and my

4. Kouzes, J. M., & Posner, B. Z. (2007). *The leadership challenge* (4th ed.). San Francisco: Jossey-Bass.

companies according to this precept and its practical value has been affirmed over and over. As we say at LifePilot, "when your values are clear, your decisions become easier." It was the clarity I had about what I stood for, my values, which helped me through the times in the early eighties that saw my net-worth drop from $150 million to negative $70 million virtually over night. It was my values that helped me through the greatest personal loss in my life when my son, Todd, took is own life in 2000. Indeed, it is in being able to survive and draw wisdom from these experiences that have revealed for me the critical importance of personal values. I realized too that offering myself as a mentor is a vital way of giving-back. It is a mutually beneficial relationship since I derive joy and meaning from it, too. In fact, it has transformed my life from success to significance. Nothing compares to knowing that you've made a difference in someone else's life, or a group of people, a city or country, or the world for that matter. I have learned that it is this practice of values-based leadership and social entrepreneurship - contributing to the enhancement of people's lives and professions, organizations and communities – that has enduring value. I consider it an honor to have had great entrepreneurial and life success and thereby the means to make a difference.

As a dedicated mentor, I'd like to leave you with the following thoughts: Be individuals of integrity first and foremost and find balance in your lives. It is critical to identify and keep your core values in front of you at all times (record them in writing) before saying yes to anything so that your choices align with your values. Be passionate - be and do your best every single day without exception. Don't ever settle for mediocrity from yourself or others. And lastly, irrespective of the difficulties in life, which will inevitably come your way, never give up, be positive always, and remember: "It's easy, it's a piece of cake!"

Best wishes,

Peter H. Thomas

Chairman Emeritus, Entrepreneurs' Organization
Vice-Chairman, Collegiate Entrepreneurs' Organization
Founder & Chairman, LifePilot
Chairman, Todd Thomas Institute for Values-Based Leadership at Royal Roads University
Chairman, Thomas Foundation (Canada) & Todd Thomas Foundation (USA)
Founder, Century 21 Real-Estate Canada Ltd. & Samoth Capital Corporation

Introduction

MENTORS

"When the disciple is ready, the master will arrive." In the following stories, as each young individual tells his unique journey of the evolution of his business, these thirteen young entrepreneurs also give a strong testament to the truth of that ancient proverb. Without a doubt, at a certain juncture of the journey, when each one of these young entrepreneurs demonstrated his own readiness, a person who had already walked the same path did appear as a guide, a mentor, and, for a time, these two walked together. It was within simple conversations shared at this juncture of the journey that each of these young entrepreneurs realized the wisdom of one who had successfully walked the path previously. Ironically, the wisdom gleaned during these conversations did not necessarily provide the lessons necessary for learning how to become the better, more successful businessman, but rather, these conversations did provide the lessons necessary for learning how to become the better man who would learn to run a more successful business.

Certainly, the student who is presently reading this introduction and who has the same aspirations as those students who are giving the accounts that will follow, has many questions, and will have many others. Among these questions are two that are most necessary for understanding the intention of this particular book. The first question is probably the most basic for taking the initial vision of the student entrepreneur to the level beyond vision and toward reality. That question is, "What does readiness mean?"

Based on the experiences storied in the pages that follow, the image of one who is ready is not one of a young student sitting poised, pen in hand or computer on knees, ready to take notes on what to do. If that is the image that readiness conjures, it is the wrong image. All wrong. The ready disciple is one who has already moved, acted, planned, ventured, risked, sweated. Nowhere in the story is the young entrepreneur waiting. In business, the word *readiness* is synonymous with the word *accomplished.* The accomplishment of the student is the invitation that a mentor anticipates before he begins to journey with the young entrepreneur. In this scenario, when the "disciple" has accomplished even a very small accomplishment, the "master" will arrive. Precisely at, and only at, that moment.

The second question is just as important, "Who is the master?" Or more directly, "How will I recognize the master, the one to whom I should attach my labors that built my dream?" The answer to that question or those questions is very simple. According to the accounts of the individuals telling the stories in this book, the answer is, Be open. The master assumes many guises. The wisdom of the successful entrepreneur is not always dressed in a dark suit, or sitting at the head of a mahogany table. It is sometimes met at a convention, or behind the sewing machine, or at the family breakfast table. In a sense, the ready student entrepreneur and the master recognize one another, and the journey begins.

What is the amazing detail of these stories is that in helping the student complete his own journey, the mentor is, at the same time, completing his own. As it is the beginning of the most meaningful part of one journey, mentoring is the completion of perhaps the most meaningful part of another. "When the disciple is ready, the master will come." And so it happens.

— MICHAEL J. MCMYNE

Student
Entrepreneurs

Joe Keeley

Winner of the *2003 Global Student Entrepreneur Awards,* Joe Keeley is the President & CEO of **College Nannies & Tutors,** the franchisor of the nation's largest nanny and tutor resource.

College Nannies & Tutors was founded by Keeley in 2001 while he was earning a degree in entrepreneurship from the University of St. Thomas in St. Paul, MN. Since GSEA, **College Nannies & Tutors** has expanded its Midwest locations to include locations on both coasts.

Joe Keeley's successful business endeavors have been rewarded. Keeley has been named one of the "Top 25 under 25 to Watch" by *Business Week Magazine,* one of the "20 under 30 Who Will Change the World" by *Citizen Culture* magazine, and one of the *Minneapolis–St. Paul Business Journal's* "40 under 40." Outside of his business ventures, Keeley serves as President of the

Minneapolis–St. Paul chapter of the Entrepreneurs' Organization (www.eonetwork.org) and volunteers his time with organizations focused on the advancement of entrepreneurship including Best-Prep, Junior Achievement, WomenVenture, and Entrepreneurs' Organization. Joe Keeley is a frequent guest lecturer at universities across the United States. Keeley resides in St. Paul, MN with his wife and daughter.

Nurturing the Internal Fire

The great thing about being a student entrepreneur is that the "bar" is set laughably low. Please allow me to explain as this statement is not intended to belittle the accomplishments of my fellow student entrepreneurs. In fact, as I continue to be humbled by the significance of the companies born in dorm rooms, my intention is quite the opposite. This "bar" or "benchmark" that I speak of is my expectation level of the student body in general. It appears that anything a student does above and beyond waking, jumping into sweatpants, consuming a balanced breakfast of cold pizza and Red Bull® and showing up for class is viewed as extraordinary. Ah, the memories... So, if my observation is indeed the standard, then student entrepreneurs are extraordinary and should be highlighted and celebrated. However, beware. It is the above standard that can nullify the potential of even the most promising venture.

It was the spring of 2003, and I was in severe danger of getting a job. If you are a parent who is presently saving or has ever saved for a child's college education with the hopes of him or her permanently launching from the nest into becoming a self-sustaining and contributing member of society, you may be rethinking the $100,000 plus tuition bill right now. After all, a J-O-B is why we go to college, isn't it? I believe the story goes thus:

Step 1: Do well in high school and on the ACT/SAT so you can get into a choice college.

Step 2: Do well in college, so you can obtain the "Holy Grail," an unpaid internship fetching non-fat lattes for the middle manager at a Fortune 500 company.

Step 3: Add the name of the prestigious school and company to your resume, so you can land the interview.

Step 4: Interview well, so you can achieve the ultimate goal.

Step 5: Mission accomplished, gainful employment!

But wait, there's more: Not only are you gainfully employed, but you also have a full suite of benefits including health, dental, disability and even a 401K. Sounds like an impressive beginning to the American Dream, doesn't it? Sounds like something a hungry twenty-two year old could use, doesn't it? Sounds like the "safe route," doesn't it? Well, as embarrassing as it is to admit, given my "entrepreneur" title, I thought so too.

I was narrowing in on the final days of my final semester of undergraduate studies at the University of St. Thomas in St. Paul, Minnesota, and I was weeks away from graduating magna cum laude. I had majored in entrepreneurship, was the president of the entrepreneurship society club, had been featured in multiple magazine and newspaper publications and won every student entrepreneur award that was brought to my attention for the launching of my company, *College Nannies & Tutors*. *College Nannies & Tutors* was a low overhead, high margin business that was part of an immense market. The stage was set. I had happy customers, support of family and friends, and cash. Business was good, and I had every reason to forge on without looking back. So, you may ask, what was the problem? Simple, I was scared.

You see, with the bar set so low at school, I WAS viewed as extraordinary, and I WAS celebrated and rewarded. Professors used my company in projects and as case studies; the press continued to write about the "college hockey-playing nanny entrepreneur," and I was even paid for my efforts. In fact, I had actually won more money from student entrepreneurial contests and awards such as *The Global Student Entrepreneur Awards* than I had in total gross sales in my senior year! I wondered, did walking across the stage and accepting my diploma mean this was all about to end? If so, perhaps it was not too late to consider another major! I realize that this story is atypical to many entrepreneurial beginnings that are riddled with naysayers. While I had a few of those, I was predominantly surrounded by cheerleaders. This left me anxious, thinking that life without the safety net that being a student provides would leave both me and the business susceptible to the business world's critique which, as we all know, sets a much higher bar than that set for the typical student painted earlier. What if I no longer was the darling of the press? Would the business actually work and stand on its own two feet outside of the protective walls of the collegiate quad? Did my diploma mean that I no longer could use the University's computer equipment, paper, staff and connections? In short, what if I failed?! To clarify, it wasn't only the fear of the business failing that was haunting me; it was my fear of failing everyone else that concerned me so. What if I had fooled myself and everyone else along the way? They wouldn't ask for the money back, would they? I was my own worst enemy.

While I consulted many individuals for the right answer to my questions, and the answers were certainly freely dispensed, I knew that the final decision was left with me. I had analysis paralysis and needed help. I turned to one entrepreneurial mentor that was part of the original discussion around the founding of *College Nannies & Tutors* and actually suggested I consider becoming an entrepreneurship major after my sixth visit to the department looking for solutions to my startup hurdles. Dr. Jeff Cornwall, past Chair of the Department of Entrepreneurship at the University of St. Thomas and now the Director of the Center of Entrepreneurship at Belmont University in Nashville, Tennessee, became my first mentor when I was first at the helm of *College Nannies & Tutors*. Dr. Cornwall, or "Dr. C." as he was often referred to, is a unique breed in the rising discipline of entrepreneurial education. He has run a multi-million-dollar health care company and is also a distinguished academic, which gives him the "street credibility" that many professors seem to lack. As my mentor, Dr. C. did three things that I believe all good mentors do at some point along the way. He set an example, acted as a guide, and he was brutally honest.

Be an example

I believe that the "do as I say not as I do" model of parenting doesn't work with children, and, therefore, the model does not work with young adults or mature adults either. Good mentors are ones that tell you that dreams can be realized, and then they show you the way this can be done. Dr. C. helped me by being an example of how to and how not to do it. He provided an example by following his passion, staying true to his values and providing hope that in doing so, all would be "okay."

Be a guide

A guide helps you to lead and extract the answer from within, often an answer that is right in front of our eyes. Dr. C. helped guide me in my decisions in the early days of the company by asking the challenging questions. Although I am certain that he had an opinion, he never pushed his answer on me. Rather, he provided his relevant experience with the hopes that I could address a problem through a more experienced filter than I was able to do alone.

Be brutally honest

Starting and running a business is hard for anyone, let alone a student with no capital, limited experience, and coursework responsibilities. Dr. C. helped mentor me by balancing the truths of the highs and lows of the entrepreneurial roller-coaster. He shared in my enthusiasm as the others did, but he was also quick to administer proper doses of reality with stories of cash flow, vendor relations, and employee issues.

It turns out that Dr. C., and apparently everyone else, knew that I was not yet finished with the journey of my business. I recall sitting face to face with a recruiter for a Fortune 500 company that was seeking an "entrepreneurial" candidate for a highly sought-after position just weeks before graduation. This was it. The position offered everything and more that would be the perfect topper to my university career. I sat down for the interview, and, to my surprise, he had an article that was written about my company stapled to my resume. "I've got this in the bag," I thought to myself as I looked at the polished HR veteran. I was ready. Bring on the classic interview questions! My strengths and weaknesses? No problem. Examples of leadership? Sure, how many would you like? However, much to my surprise, he opened with a very unorthodox zinger. "Tell me, Joe, why would you want to leave running your own business to work for a multi-national, multi-billion-dollar company where I can guarantee that you will not have much autonomy for the first five years?" While the question was certainly not one that I was prepared for, it was the fire in his eyes that struck me the most. It seemed that from behind his cushy salary, pressed suit, company car and benefit package that would make any small business owner blush, there was a hint of desire, even jealousy. Perhaps he had a business idea that he hatched daily in his head or once dreamed of forging his own path, but for one likely legitimate and sensible reason or another, he chose a different path. It was almost like he, like everyone else, was cheering me on in his own way to jump feet first into the business. He knew, and more importantly I knew, that I was not made for the corporate world. I was an entrepreneur, and there was no hiding that fact.

It has been over five years since I was wavering on the edge of employment, and I can honestly say that the challenges and dilemmas of entrepreneuership have not gone away. In fact, they have only increased in scale and quantity. The highs and lows of being an entrepreneur have brought franchise offices in sixteen states, hundreds of employees, mortgages and a family, all very good things, but none without risk, stress and big decisions. I can't help but smile to think of how in a college dorm, I lamented over what now seems like such an easy decision. However, that is the thing about being an entrepreneur; we are forced to make important decisions each and every day. It is lonely at the top, and there is no road map. To help the novice navigate the unknown is precisely why mentors are so important. They provide a sense of calm in the storm and protect us from what is the single greatest obstacle that can jeopardize an entrepreneurial venture, the entrepreneur.

Michael Kopko

Michael Kopko's impressive academic credentials serve to enhance his already impressive business resume. Michael Kopko graduated from Harvard in 2007, with an honors degree in economics. Presently, he is pursuing an MBA at Columbia University's Graduate School of Business. Michael Kopko is the recipient of the Feldberg Fellowship, a full tuition merit scholarship honoring the former Dean Feldberg and sponsored by Henry Kravis. However, even before earning these academic credentials and experience, in the fall of 2003, during his first semester on campus and in his dorm room, Michael founded **DormAid LLC. DormAid** is the nation's leading market maker for college services. The company currently provides laundry, cleaning, water delivery, computer back-up, appliances, and a variety of other services to college students. To promote his business, Michael has made numerous appearances in major media outlets including Fox News, *The New York Times,* Comedy Central's *The Daily Show,* and MSNBC's *Scarborough Country.* He has been named one of New York City's "Wunderkinds" and one of *Scene Magazine's* "15 Most Interesting Harvard Students." In the 2007 New England Regional Finals competition, The GSEA organization awarded **DormAid** the *Global Student Entrepreneur Awards* and placed the company in the top six finalists in its Global Competition. Outside of the business arena, Michael enjoys reading, exercising, and flying planes.

There are businesses that you develop yourself, and there are businesses that you stumble upon. For me, it might be more appropriate to say that in 2004, I stumbled over a company that manifested itself as a pile of dirty clothes on my dorm room's floor. As a freshman at Harvard, all I wanted was a clean room. Indeed, the process of acclimating myself to college life, making friends, and still focusing on classes left little time to keep my things tidy. After some thought, I found myself interviewing potential cleaners for my roommate and myself. One thing led to another, and quickly thereafter, I was organizing cleanups on behalf of many of the residents of my building. That month's accumulation of dirty clothes wafted in not only a pungent mixture of sweat and cologne but also an idea for a new business. As business grew, my father became somewhat frightened that the son he had sent off to get an education was spending his time teaching kids how to clean. From my perspective, I was simply giving people what they wanted.

In fact, establishing *DormAid* was not at all about cleaning hundreds of rooms, folding thousands of bags of laundry, shipping appliances and bedding, offering water delivery, or providing career advice. It began as a political process when Harvard rejected my request to start a room cleaning business on campus. Determined and stubborn, I did not even consider accepting their verdict and started a long process of appealing their decision. Looking back, I spent most of my sophomore year the way any political interest group does: building coalitions to support the approval of my business.

After battling Harvard's administration for the better part of nine months, victory finally seemed imminent. That sense was short lived. The University's publication, *The Harvard Crimson*, ran an editorial that jeopardized all the work that I had done. The article called for Harvard students to boycott my company, then called *DorMaid*, suggesting it was a divisive service with a sexist name. I was saddened because I thought I had finally won my right to run the business, and now, I had to deal with *The Harvard Crimson*. However, what was certainly one of the most stressful times in my life, and in the life of my company, was actually a blessing in disguise.

As I was leaving an accounting exam at MIT in February of 2005, I received a phone call from a reporter at Reuters who asked me if I had any comment regarding Harvard's boycott. I explained that I was frustrated that *The Crimson* was trying to take choice away from people by suggesting we should not be given approval to operate.

> *"In a free economy it's all about choice, and the Crimson is trying to take choice away from people," the student entrepreneur told Reuters. "I think it's a very uneconomic and narrow view. It's essentially against creating wealth for society."*

This perhaps was the most important interview of my life as the story ran across the nation. Soon, radio stations, *The New York Times,* Comedy Central's *The Daily Show,* and more media organizations were calling me. The company's name changed, and *DormAid's* story was being heard coast to coast. Rush Limbaugh even suggested that I should be given a professorship instead of being punished: "This guy should be named a professor, he seems to me to have already graduated most business schools." With all of this attention came great people who wanted to join *DormAid* and help it grow. It was at that moment that I knew my job was no longer about cleaning rooms, but about building a business that could both bring college students together and provide them with useful services.

The story of how the *DormAid* team, all under twenty-two years old, was able to both cram for final exams and meet with lawyers to discuss the inevitable threat of intellectual property lawsuits during the same thirty minutes while still juggling to be as "normal" as possible is a noteworthy one. Picture the thrills of making the first $100,000, the tears of acute mental breakdowns, the crankiness after a library all-nighter, the rioting of a college night… In short, how a company that Fox News noted to be as "ambitious as Wal-Mart" was being built exclusively by college undergraduates seems almost fictional.

The lessons I have learned from taking a cleaning service to the nation's leading college service provider have been intensely valuable to me. I am glad to share them with the next generation of entrepreneurs, so they don't have to spend the time and resources I did learning these lessons all over again. Looking back, I am still amazed that I kept fighting for *Dorm-Aid's* right to live on, especially over such a niche idea. From my understanding of people with "great ideas," the greatest difference between entrepreneurs and non-entrepreneurs is that non-entrepreneurs never actually give it a try.

There are three core problems that prevent people from ever getting their ideas off the ground. First, entrepreneurs are not focused on the downside—they are focused on the upside. Though they are often wrong, fear is the last thing on their mind. Entrepreneurship can even be lonely—in many cases you must remain a misunderstood artist as you are bringing something to the world that it has never seen before. I remember the *DormAid* team watching an episode of Showtime's *Bullsh*t* about a company called *Neuticle,* which implants fake testicles into neutered dogs for the owners' sociological comfort. We started making fun of the entrepreneur for having such a dumb idea. We soon learned he had sold over 600,000 pairs of fake dog testicles. Silence swallowed our laughter as we realized we hadn't sold that many of anything yet. We felt as incompetent as one of the dogs the man was discussing.

Second, you need to jump without a parachute. I don't mean to suggest that entrepreneurs should be unprepared, but taking visible and tangible risks lets employees know that the venture must succeed. Necessity is often the greatest generator of innovation, and individuals often become teams behind mutually shared risks. Entrepreneurs can run businesses in their spare time but these should be considered more like sole proprietorships or hobbies rather than businesses. Bold moves are very important to establishing a psychology of success. The *DormAid* team's bold move came when we resigned from Harvard Student Agencies (HSA), a company we had been working for in early 2005. The decision came one August day after our boss informed us of the importance of sweeping the floor each morning and the best techniques for doing so (this is not a joke). We decided then and there that it was time to jump. Changing the world had to become a full time job for us rather than a nighttime hobby that we participated in after work. Resigning was not easy, and HSA, in fact, threatened us with litigation. It was all nonsense, of course, the flailing of a big business that thought it could intimidate young kids. At the end of the day, HSA could not bring us down and, in fact, served only to bring us closer together—like brothers.

Third, entrepreneurs need to understand that the journey to success is a long and winding road. Success is something that you feel each day, something that is internally derived and, occasionally, externally reinforced. If you are coming to entrepreneurship because you think you will make millions in no time then you are likely in for disappointing results. Part of entrepreneurship is, if anything, valuing change and achievement over money. There are better risk-adjusted ways to make money than in entrepreneurship. I find that the most successful entrepreneurs envision a change that they are committed to achieving regardless of the obstacles, consequences, and financial struggles that lay in wait.

Though starting a business is often the hold up for many entrepreneurs, turning their idea into a functioning and sustainable business is equally challenging. One of the techniques I have found to be most effective is the use of mentors. We were young entrepreneurs lacking the experience and relationships that can make doing business easier and less risky. The most important advice I received when I was at Harvard came from a man by the name of Bill Wright-Swadell, who was the head of Harvard's Office of Career Services. He explained the importance of building a personal board of directors: "You are surrounded by people who care about you, are very accomplished, and want to see you succeed. Take advantage of that." I believed Mr. Swadell, and upon *DormAid's* founding, I decided to recruit an advisory board that would guide us through the world of business. I also sought out a personal mentor as well to help coach me as I built the business. Mentors are particularly important for entrepreneurs because these leaders often lack the advisors that exist naturally in big businesses. After a month of emails and follow-ups, we had recruited eight fine individuals who offered their advice and guidance to us.

The advisory board helped me accomplish some important benchmarks. First, it helped me escape the biggest problem I faced: I was expected to lead a group of people who were smarter than me. To me, leadership meant growth, and enabling people to become better and enriched. I knew immediately that I was going to need serious help. Second, the advisory board enabled us to suggest that the company was not run by a bunch of sophomores and juniors in college, but by wise and experienced businessmen and businesswomen. Though we were proud of our youth and our precociousness, mothers would probably not consider it an added bonus that those who were serving their children were their children's age. Finally, the advisory board helped us establish a community around the company and create structure. We included members in our meetings once a month and even stayed with some of them when we had to travel across the country marketing.

We have learned many things from our advisors as well. John Foley taught us to ask questions like: Who is our buyer? How should we design our website and marketing materials to optimize our conversion rates? Rakesh Kaul taught us that bumble bees don't scale because if you increased the size of the bumble bee by 1000 times the wings would never support the mass of the bumble bee. In that same way we had to learn that we should not expect to linearly scale our systems if we wanted to grow. And finally, Gary Berman taught that including hugs in our lives and caring about our people would be essential for the business to succeed.

In addition to the formal advisory board structure, I decided to seek out a personal mentor in July of 2006. I wrote a letter to George David, the CEO of United Technologies,[1] who I had met at a few events previously and asked if he would meet with me a few times a year to help me become a better leader. I was so grateful to receive a correspondence from him letting me know that he had accepted my request and was willing to meet with me.

The goal of my first meeting at the Waldorf Astoria was to get a second one. At the end of the meeting I asked Mr. David what he would have me do before our next meeting, and he recommended a "few books" that I read. The next day I received a package in Cambridge with three books totaling over 2,000 pages. The reading was intense, mostly about American and Siberian history, but it helped me realize something very important: leaders need to be great historians. Mr. David considers himself a historian, explaining, "I have been here for a long time and I know most of the things we have done.

---

1. George David was of the CEO of United Technologies from 1994 to 2008. He added more than $50 billion of shareholder value during his tenure there.

When someone comes to me with an idea we have already tried before, my job is to ask them why they think times are different now."

There are two other pieces of advice that I remember very well from our time together. One is, it is important to understand a system rather than to memorize isolated facts. "Everything you learn you need to learn by comprehension, not memory." The second piece of advice is about leadership. I asked Mr. David what his philosophy on CEO likeability was, and he described two ends of a spectrum. On one side of the spectrum was General Patton's philosophy: the hard-charging, aggressive, and often abusive leader. On the other end of the spectrum are leaders who trade rewards for love. These leaders often give promotions and jobs to people within their group and may not bring in outside talent. He explained that his metaphor was the hot tub. "I think it is important to be respected, but you (Mr. David's employee) will do your job, and I will not be in that hot tub with you if you don't." Mr. David is an "Emersonian" who focuses on increasing the responsibility of his people and holding them accountable for their actions. He likes to see the backs of his employee's heads as they are off working without constantly needing input from him. He believes in giving managers their own financial statements and holding them as accountable for the results as possible.

My relationship with Mr. David has enabled me to think about leadership, management, and business building from a higher perspective. In my last meeting with him in Hartford, I visited him in his top floor office suite and was lucky enough to fly back to New York City with him in his helicopter. It was a quick 30-minute flight right into the city, a trip that had taken me two and a half hours to do by Amtrak. As we hovered in the air I soaked in his greatest message, "Always seek the highest elevation." I had traveled by train, but he was returning by helicopter. My vantage point was of course a borrowed perch, but it helped me realize the existence of a higher point than where I stood. Entrepreneurs need to remember that they are surrounded by great mountains on all sides, and in order to understand the structure of the world they play in, they need to seek "the view from 100,000 feet."

There is a great deal of advice that people throw at budding entrepreneurs, and one important skill set we inevitably develop is to say thank you and continue down our path. If I could do this all over again, I would establish two principles early on in the process. The first would be to solve interesting problems, and the second would be to recruit, attract, and develop top talent. Hard problems keep teams engaged, and their solutions can contribute to society in surprising ways. As you contemplate starting your adventure or taking it to the next level, make sure to clearly define what problem you are trying to solve and make sure your leadership is focused on solving it. Strip away the managerial minutia that is best left to large corporations and focus on your solution. Always remember that your safety net is very large. Our society encourages risk taking, and there is no reason, especially when you are young, not to give it a try.

Tim Hamilton

Tim Hamilton is the founder and president of *Astonish Designs*, a web-based software development firm based in Austin, Texas. In the year 2000, while still in high school, Tim began the company as a means of accelerating his education in software design and development. While attending the University of Texas at Austin, Tim expanded *Astonish Designs* to include the city of Houston, Mrs. Grossman's Paper Company, and RICOH Americas. Building on this success, in 2003, Tim co-founded with Houston-based startup, *Anatom-e Information Systems,* a revolutionary medical information system for cancer diagnosis. In 2005, Tim co-founded *OpenTeams,* a Software-as-a-Service company that, through its groundbreaking collaboration methodology, aimed at promoting innovation and creativity. Tim's success continued, and, in 2007, Tim was a finalist in the Global Student Entrepreneur Awards competition. Tim

has since become an active member of E.O. Accelerator, an organization whose primary purpose is to assist in the development of
young entrepreneurs.

I t was 4:30 AM, and my work was complete. My client sat
slumped over and asleep in the office chair next to me. My
heart beat rapidly as I imagined the success of my first project.
I proudly placed my name at the bottom of the poster that had
emerged over the past ten hours, and I sat back to admire it.
I was on fire.

I had discovered Adobe Photoshop only a few months
prior and had spent virtually every free moment practicing
techniques and scouring the internet for design tutorials. I ate
lunch in my high school library as I poured over articles about
bezier curves and drop shadows. I had mastered flaming let-
ters and psychedelic lighting effects, but what I really wanted
was a project.

This poster was my first project, and Jesse Cooper, my tennis coach, used it to market his annual tennis tournament.
After hearing about my Photoshop obsession during tennis
practice earlier in the week, Jesse became my first client, and,
I thus began my entrepreneurial journey.

With Jesse's guidance, I designed forty posters and three websites. I named my company *Astonish Designs,* and, having three clients, I earned $1,100 in the first year. Christmas came early that year, and my parents invested $600 to pay for web hosting and a copy of Photoshop. I was fifteen, knew a bit of HTML and was ready to take on the world with a keyboard and mouse. Reflecting on those early projects, one thing is clear; I was passionate about creating. Even as a child, nothing excited me more than a project. In *E-Myth Mastery,* a powerful, insightful book about entrepreneurship, Michael Gerber writes, "Creation, the act of producing something out of nothing, the love that one finds in the pure act of it, is enough to last a human being a lifetime."

I had just discovered that joy, and I was hooked. With nothing in my way, I sought larger projects and bigger challenges. As I acquired more clients, I was forced to broaden my abilities to keep up with their changing needs. To accelerate my learning, I needed access to industry professionals.

In May of 2000, I called a local web development firm. With false confidence, I introduced myself and explained that I was looking for a summer internship. Dave Nienberg, the owner, was audibly doubtful. He told me to call back in a week and warned me that it was unlikely. We spoke a week later and set up an interview. I presented my resume, albeit short, and answered questions about my strengths, weaknesses and career interests. After an hour, I was hired and introduced to the team.

After spending two summers interning there, I learned four programming languages and saw how proposals, contracts and invoices were created. My co-workers stayed after hours to teach me about database theory, programming and server management, and I fell in love with every aspect of the business. I loved the sound of the server-room and was inspired as I witnessed creative professionals moving projects through each stage of their life cycle. This was definitely the business for me.

In 2002, having just graduated from high school, I spent the summer designing marketing materials for a distributor of allergy and asthma relief products. During the day I worked with Dean Petrosewicz, the president, promoting and designing new product lines. Dean gave me free reign over his marketing department. I designed catalogs, brochures, trade show displays and product labels. He funded every idea I had, and together, we stimulated a sizable increase in third and fourth quarter sales. Dean taught me to document everything, how to speak with confidence and how to read a financial statement. Perhaps the most valuable lesson I learned from Dean was to prepare at least one recommendation before approaching anyone with a problem.

In the spring of 2003, my father introduced me to George Danner, a business consultant who used computer modeling to help companies solve large strategic problems. I was studying computer science at the University of Texas at the time, and my dad thought George could pass on some valuable advice. We met for lunch, and my jaw dropped as I watched George's animated simulations churning through vast data sets, processing complex scenarios and creating clairvoyant forecasts. Much to my surprise, George offered me an internship that summer. This internship was a remarkable opportunity with a front row seat to witness the marriage of business and science with bursts of game theory and econometrics. Together, we built a model to support a 500-million-dollar decision for an ocean-operating logistics company. George is not only brilliant, but he is also incredibly generous. He taught me to think analytically, entrusted me with his customers and nurtured my entrepreneurial spirit.

In the fall of 2003 (I was now studying economics at university) I spent a year working with a startup on a medical imaging system for diagnostic radiologists. I devoted half of my time to this endeavor and the other half to *Astonish Designs,* working on a growing number of websites. By the end of the year, we had completed a prototype that intelligently mapped volumes of medical information to a patient's real anatomy as seen in an MRI scan, for example. The result was a three-dimensional human anatomy whose organs were interactively cross-referenced to a massive medical database. While the product was incredibly well-received by prospective customers, we failed as an organization. Interpersonal dynamics hindered our collaboration, and eventually, those dynamics resulted in the collapse of the company. This was a devastating experience that taught me the value of open communication and the importance of level-headed management.

The experience also refocused me on *Astonish Designs,* the only place where I was in full control of my time. With renewed concentration, I attracted a few key customers, outsourced replaceable processes and expanded our services to grow a source of recurring revenue. In 2004, I hired a full-time developer, and together, we went head-on with a growing number of complex projects. I could feel it in the pit of my stomach...we were on the verge of a breakthrough.

In the summer of 2005, George Danner introduced me to Tory Gattis, a visionary thought-leader in the area of management and corporate innovation. Tory and I met over dinner in downtown Austin to discuss his vision. Tory's plan was to create a software product that would replace email as the primary collaboration tool for business teams. The product he envisioned would break down the walls of bureaucracy, harness creativity and engage employees.

As the night progressed, we uncovered a powerful synergy as we shared ideas and explored concepts. This would surely be a phenomenal collaboration. A few weeks later, Tory gave us the green light and thus began our most fruitful, albeit formidable, undertaking. At that time, *Astonish* was a company of two, but we embraced the project fearlessly. In May 2007, after two years of analysis, design and development, *OpenTeams* emerged, and it was beautiful. From a technical perspective, *OpenTeams* was on the bleeding edge. As far as we could tell, our application was the only one of its kind with an unrivaled user interface and groundbreaking workflow. Our launch attracted an impressive amount of early adopters as bloggers reviewed and praised the application.

OpenTeams taught me that we could solve big problems. With Tory's support, we turned his grand vision into a digital reality. We leveraged a virtual team of developers and designers, which laid the groundwork for the outsourcing practices that we use today. Occasionally, our team met up in-person to hammer out a big milestone, sometimes working for 24 hours straight. While this was physically exhausting, it was just as inspiring as I witnessed the shear strength of the human spirit when properly motivated. The team was galvanized by Tory's unwavering commitment to his lifelong entrepreneurial dream, a model of inspirational leadership that I will never forget.

In the meantime, *Astonish Designs* had grown into a team of three local employees and a worldwide network of full-time and part-time contractors. We had over one hundred clients ranging from manufacturing to professional services. I closed my home-based office and moved the company into an office building nestled in the trees of central Austin. Our work on *OpenTeams* had attracted a number of consulting projects, which supplemented our web design and hosting business. In the year that followed, we doubled annual revenue for the seventh time, created a financial reporting system for the City of Houston and pioneered a dispatch and logistics technology for SCI, the world's largest funeral home company.

In retrospect, it is clear to me that this journey began long before the days of posters and websites. In all truth, it began at home. I was raised in a supportive household with an emphasis on integrity and discipline. My parents nurtured my creativity and allowed me the freedom to explore the endless possibilities of my imagination. While investing generously in my education, they remained patient and understanding as my ambitions occasionally distracted me from my school work. They were behind me from the very beginning, never doubting even my wildest dreams.

None of this would have been possible without the people that supported and guided me along the way. These are the people that helped me build *Astonish Designs* into the living, breathing business I had vividly imagined as a child. Miraculously, that one poster project was enough to set the pendulum in motion. However, the fuel of my business, what has kept me going all this time, came from all the people that gave me a chance. My brave employees that took a job with no guarantee, my daring clients that put their project on the line and my kind mentors that gave so generously of their time and experience.

Joseph A. Pascaretta

Joseph A. Pascaretta established not one, but two successful firms specializing in two completely different industries. The focus of one of the businesses was internet technology and software development, while the other focused on horticultural services. Before establishing his business, Joseph had to establish professional relationships with clients who were older and more experienced. Earning the trust of these individuals required Joseph to take his strategies a step further when approaching the task of developing a business relationship. These extra steps included enhancing the level of professionalism and keeping an accurate reference list. Another obstacle that had to be overcome was the warnings from older, more experienced businessmen that a business endeavor would require too much time and interfere with Joseph's education. However, Joseph turned these warnings into motivation. In

June of 2008, at the age of twenty, Joseph A. Pascaretta, chairman and CEO, received the ***Ernst & Young's Entrepreneur of the Year Award*** in the category of products and solutions. In addition to establishing and running his businesses, Joseph is a motivational speaker, private pilot, and a student of business and economics at the University of Michigan.

Even in 1999, when my business partner, Aaron D. Dowen, and I were eleven years of age, we knew that the keys to any successful venture were dedication and innovation. It was then that the Alps family of companies began. Guided by Aaron's gift for computer programming, we produced our first website, which included a database of airplane pictures. Eventually, we decided to sell a site to our first customer in the construction industry. Going into that first sales meeting with the directors of the company was one of the most difficult challenges we had ever faced in our young lives. Upon arrival into the meeting room, there was a wave of laughter at two pre-teen boys in suits lugging a rented projector, diagrams and perspectives. However, Aaron and I were one step ahead of these directors. We had already put together a website which would allow them to see exactly what we were selling. In addition, we implemented features such as a flash and certain HTML functions that were new to the internet technology world. Since I always considered myself the "sales person" of the partnership, I delivered the presentation. After one hour of speaking, I opened the floor to questions. There was silence. The first person who spoke was the president of the company who loved the design. It soon became apparent that not only the president, but also the directors who were present at the meeting were impressed with our hard work.

As eleven-year-olds, our resources were limited, but our spirit was determined. With money saved from cutting lawns, we were able to purchase the necessary website development software. However, naming the company was another task. We wanted something that directly described our work ethic as well as our relationship with our customers. Our goal was to provide our customers with the best services and products possible. With the desire to communicate this message, Alps technology was born.

Once we were able to secure our first deal, we were able to retain some of our earnings, invest in commodities, and invest back into the company. With this strategy, in two years, the company grew from two to twelve employees. Alps was moving on a solid track. In 2001, our newly founded board of directors decided to invest in purchasing and maintaining our own database systems. This decision allows us to maintain websites for a broader customer base—automotive dealerships, large construction firms, and industrial companies.

We have always attributed our success to our foundation principles:

The Alps Key to Success List

- Recognizing Potential Investments & Innovating Industry Standards
- Establishing Strong Cliental Base
- Maintaining Superior Level of Professionalism
- Delivering Products/Services = Results
- Success = Leaders + Motivation
- Time Management Proficiency

The year 2002 presented us with another challenge. We noticed a downfall in the demand for website development. Accepting this challenge, within six months our associates strategically developed a new service: providing hardware, software, and consulting for companies. This adjustment allowed us to meet the needs of smaller companies who do not have the capability of supporting an onsite technological division. In addition, Aaron and I began a joint venture, The Alps Lawn Company. This was a company in the landscape and horticultural service industry. With a completely different clientele base, Aaron and I faced new challenges of targeting specific customers. With innovation and strategic marketing programs, we were successful in targeting executive estates and larger residential developments. In the larger commercial sector, Alps targets larger office complexes, municipal organizations, and educational facilities. Even though the two branches of the Alps companies are very different, the marketing strategies between both Alps companies are very similar. The number one focus of both branches is customer satisfaction.

The key to success with this company was that Aaron and I learned every aspect of landscape management. Our first year in business, we cut the grass, read landscape literature, and relied on the expertise of other landscape professionals. Like the Alps Technology International, The Alps Lawn Company utilizes the latest technology.

The Alps Lawn Company

- Our Supervisors utilize the latest IT technology—they use Blackberry devices so clients can send e-mail instead of calling—We have GPS trackers on all of our vehicles and equipment, so we know where everything is 24/7.
- We offer online payment programs where clients can check accounts and make payments via a login through our

website—this is revolutionary in the landscape/horticultural industry.

• We offer complementary aerial photography—clients get a "bird's eye view" of their properties.

• Along with Alps Technology, we have developed Computer Aided Design Landscape design software to allow customers to view a "before" image of their property, then an "after" shot with the new landscaping. This is revolutionary to the landscape industry, as most companies show a "blue-print" design and clients have to "imagine" what it would look like. With Alps, you can see EXACTLY how our projects will result.

• Our equipment/vehicles are cleaned daily—giving us the most professional appearance.

• We use only the newest equipment—3 years old or newer, resulting in less down time.

• Our garages/warehouses resemble dealerships—epoxy-coated floors that are cleaned daily.

In 2008, Alps took yet another direction. The Alps Holding Group was founded as a holding company that would manage the assets of Alps Technology and The Alps Lawn Company, while providing investment services and consulting. It was shortly thereafter that the board of directors decided that it was time to merge the three companies into one enterprise—Alps International. I was named the Chairman of the Board, as well as the Chief Executive Officer, with Aaron Dowen being named Chief Financial Officer and President. In addition, we integrated a new customer care center in Portland, Oregon.

However, none of my success would have been possible had it not been for Lawrence J. Ellison. Lawrence J. Ellison, founder of Oracle Corporation, has been my mentor. Founding Oracle in 1977, Ellison began working with the government, as it worked on a forefront database software project. This software project was well ahead of its time. Oracle was developed as one of the most professional and advanced database corporations in the world.

Another very important aspect of business is making ethical decisions and giving back to the community. Each summer, all of the Michigan-based employees from Alps Technology International and The Alps Lawn Company are given a three-day weekend, where we work at the United Urban Foundation, a local organization that constructs homes for the less fortunate. Over this weekend, we not only learn about the people we work with everyday, but we also grow as a team, helping both the community and struggling families. In addition to our volunteer time of approximately 50 hours, The Alps Lawn Company contributes approximately $25,000 in landscaping supplies/material to help beautify the homes. Our employees have a great sense of satisfaction when contributing the "final touch" of the home. In addition to building individual character within our employee and management environment, I know each employee benefits greatly from this business-community event. Everyone must work as a team to produce the final outcome—and that is the home. It is rewarding for them to see the smile of the family that will reside in this newly constructed home. It is also rewarding for me to watch our employees grow as citizens of the community.

Also, I am a Notre Dame Preparatory graduate, so the company regularly donates select landscape management services each year. I feel Notre Dame Preparatory was my foundation to a successful business career, so I am more than happy to donate.

The most valuable advice I could give to any aspiring entrepreneur is to really enjoy the field he or she is pursuing. In order for any successful organization to grow, the founders must be in it for the right reasons. When I motivationally speak for educational institutions, the students typically ask me about salaries and pay for our employees. This is not why Aaron and I have joined the industries in which we innovate. We have always had a passion for success, innovation and technological integration. We enjoy working each day with the organizations that we are a part of. We have been fortunate enough to receive the prestigious Ernst & Young Entrepreneur of the Year in 2008 for our business efforts and achievements. This is not only substantial motivation to pursue advancement within our industries, but is a real complement to us for our efforts.

What makes our story unique is that we established not one but two companies in two completely different industries—internet technology/software development and the horticultural service industry. In addition to running the businesses, I am a motivational speaker, private pilot, and I am graduating from the University of Michigan three semesters early. Over the course of founding the businesses, we have faced many obstacles and barriers including establishing professional relationships with corporate clients and getting them to do business with a younger person. From enhancing the level of professionalism to keeping a solid reference list, we really had to take everything a step further when approaching a deal. Many people who we considered as being role models have told us to sell the businesses because the responsibilities would interfere with our school demands. However, Aaron and I turned their comments of caution into motivation.

My vision as an executive with both Alps companies is to further innovate the industries in which we are involved.

For Alps Technology International, it is to continue to work alongside Fortune 500 companies to innovate the healthcare industry. We will offer our clients the latest consulting/IT services within the industry. I would like us to grow larger in the Asian and European markets, exposing us to some phenomenal international potential. I would also like not only to keep our constant growth rate, but also to increase it. For The Alps Lawn Company, I would like to see us become a national firm continuing to innovate the industry by offering our clients the latest technology, utilizing it within the landscape/horticultural service sector to build on its success by building on the half-million dollar contracts that we have been awarded.

Being an entrepreneur is not a nine-to-five job—it requires real dedication, passion, ambition, and motivation. There are still times I work seven days a week—however, I enjoy each minute of it. Business and entrepreneurs are the future. My advice would be not to listen to people who tell you it is impossible to begin and run a business. In addition to a strong work ethic, I recommend pursuing a career that interests you, the entrepreneur. You have to have a passion for what you do. I know that's been said a million times, but if you want to be successful, that advice is true. The advice that has not been stated a million times, and even if it had been, would still not be a cliché, but would rather be the most compelling advice that any young entrepreneur could ever have is simple: Find a mentor. Once a mentoring relationship has been established, then simply observe, listen and learn.

Andrew Cavitolo

Andrew Cavitolo is the founder and creator of ***Three Guys and a Girl, LLC,*** a company that, under its umbrella, manufactures, markets and sells two clothing brands. Creating the company in 2005 while he was still in college, Andrew assembled partners and investors to launch his first brand, ***Nonami Premium,*** a premium denim and contemporary sportswear collection. After the success of his first season, Andrew was featured in Bloomingdale's Department Stores and boutiques nationwide. One of Nonami's initial creations, "Brooklyn Suede Pocket Denim," was featured in *Maxim Magazine*'s *Style 100, COED Magazine,* and *Entrepreneur Magazine.* Soon, however, Andrew realized that in featuring only denim, he was competing in apparel's most oversaturated market. Motivated by this realization, *Three Guys and a Girl* decided to design a complete collection of premium sportswear which did not include denim. This collection was launched under the label *Bohden James*. In this collection, Andrew and his team targeted the 20-to-35-year-old young professional. Since its debut in the spring of 2008, *Bohden James* has been featured in two of fashion industry's most impressive trade magazines where it was reviewed as "The New Generation of Sophistication," and "a Ralph Lauren with an attitude." This collection has lived up to these reviews and has carved its niche in over 60 high-end boutiques nationwide.

*B*ohden James is a high-end men's contemporary sportswear apparel company. We started selling with a pair of jeans in Bloomingdale's, and now we are a complete collection selling nationwide as well as in many other countries. Along the way, I have experienced many successes and many failures. The people that I met and the mentors that I acquired were able to help me eliminate the failures and create the success. Success did not just happen overnight. It was a struggle and one of the best learning experiences of my life.

My journey started in my junior year in college. I was studying at Fairleigh Dickinson University, and I just finished an internship working as an assistant restaurant manager for a restaurant at Bloomingdale's, the flagship location in New York City. During my internship I met many influential people that led me into my career today. Being part of the restaurant let me meet many people from different departments in the store. During my time working for Bloomingdale's, I began to take interest in the clothing industry. I was always a consumer of high-end apparel, but I thought it would be even more interesting to make my own. I made it a priority to meet the correct people in Bloomingdale's.

A couple of months into my junior year, I was sitting in my dorm room talking with my roommates when I brought up the idea of starting our own clothing line. I talked with them about the people I met during my summer internship, and my enthusiasm made my roommates jump right onto the idea. With excitement of our first business opportunity we realized one thing. Although we had a possible outlet to sell clothes, no one knew how to design or make clothes. To solve this problem, we went online, researched designers, found our first designer, and we hired him. This designer happened to have a connection with a sourcing agent to manufacture the clothes.

Our first concept was to create a tee-shirt and denim line targeting the 18-to-35-year-old consumer. We wanted to call the line *Nonami Premium* since we were specializing in Japanese premium denim. Also, since we had no name for the label, our first idea was to spell it NONAME and pronounce it "No-Nah-Mee," but that idea did not connect with people because it was hard to pronounce, so we added the "I" to the name to have the word sound like it is spelled. With a $4000 investment, we created samples. Soon afterwards, I called the executives I met during my internship at Bloomingdale's. The executives scheduled me to present my idea to three people. These three people were the most powerful men in Bloomingdale's, including David Fisher, listed as one of the Forbes top 500 most powerful people in retail. Being only three months into creating our first product and not knowing anything about the business, the idea of this meeting was a little scary for me. During the meeting, Bloomingdale's did not want to write an order because they did not trust the production nor time of delivery since we were a start-up company. It took me three hours of back-and-forth negotiating to finally convince Bloomingdale's to trust me. After the meeting, we had completed our first order of 1000 units with Bloomingdale's. This success marked one of the most exciting days of my life.

The next couple of months were spent making sure that we aligned the production to come in on time and that the product came out great for the 2006 holiday season. We acquired a loan and ordered 10,000 units of product to cover us for re-orders. Due to financial reasons, during this time I lost one of the partners in the company. This loss was a problem because we had to locate other funding sources to cover the production. Eventually, we were able to secure money, and we were set to go. We were debuting our first clothing line on retail's Good Friday, the Friday after Thanksgiving, the biggest shopping day of the year. The product came in on time, but getting it through the Bloomingdale's system to get on the shelves in time was taking longer than expected. I had to alert the associates from my internship to have my product expedited through the system process to get onto the floors. That mission was accomplished, and we debuted on November 24, 2006, in Bloomingdale's Flagship and Soho stores.

The first day we debuted we sold over $6,000 in product. It was a hit! The rest of the holiday season went by, and the product was selling extremely well, especially for a new brand. We were featured in *Maxim* magazine's top ten jeans on the market. We had a write up in *Entrepreneur Magazine, The Star Ledger, Stuff Magazine* as well as in other industry trade publications. The only problem was that despite the solid sales, Bloomingdale's was not re-ordering the product. I called the company numerous times, and they said since we are a new product they want to sell out of us first then re-order for next season. At the end of the season, they informed me that since the denim market was oversaturated, and their overall season was slow, they were going to drop some of their newer brands and focus on their core business, such as Seven Jeans and True Religion. This was devastating news to me because Bloomingdale's was a major account, and we sold well, but more devastating is that we had 9,000 units in storage. This realization is where we went into panic mode and felt it was time to get some insight from someone who was actually in this business.

For this direction, I contacted one of our first mentors, Mercedes Gonzalez. She was the owner of Global Purchasing, a buying and consulting group for the fashion industry. We met her and explained to her our situation. She knew we made the biggest mistake people make in the industry, ordering over product. Following that meeting, we met a couple of more times to help liquidate the product. We wound up liquidating the tee-shirts and denim to Daffy's. We developed a productive relationship, and Mercedes Gonzalez agreed to continue to meet to develop a new launch of product. We decided we wanted to stay in this industry with the goal of developing a great brand. Mercedes was willing to help us along the way.

After we liquidated our entire inventory, we developed the idea of a clothing line that mixes prep styles with contemporary. It was a new version of "Ralph Lauren with an attitude." We called it *Bohden James*. *Bohden James* is a lifestyle revolution. It consists of a complete collection of contemporary/prep sportswear including jackets, pants, dress shirts, polos, tees, vests, and our specialty blazers. Mercedes helped us with the design and production of the samples and helped us coordinate trade shows to help sell the product. We showed our spring 2008 collection, and it was an instant hit. With our trade show sales and traveling around to different accounts, a total of 36 stores including some big names like Rothmans, Universal Gear, Flying A, and many more picked up the *Bohden James* brand. We were selling nationwide from New York to California and even acquired a boutique in Japan at one of the trade shows.

At this point we were growing, and I asked the closest person in my life to be my next mentor. We needed to secure a financial institution to be our factor and help organize all the receivables and bills, and I did not know anyone better to ask than my mother Patricia Cavitolo. When it comes to organization she is an expert, and she also can coordinate the finances with me. She was more than happy to help, and with her knowledge we were able to acquire GMAC (a large financial institution) to factor all our receivables. We were also able to get a line of credit from the bank to help with cash flow. This financial capability put us in the right direction and situation to continue on our growth path.

With both mentors by my side, the company was moving along much better than my previous method of "winging it."

We finished our fall 2008 booking better than expected, and we were ready to launch our spring 2008 season in stores. Here, we encountered another problem with our new manufacturers. Since our orders were smaller than the other orders in the factory, we were placed on the "back burner." As a result, our orders came in over a month later than we were supposed to deliver them to our clients. Now, we were in domino effect, and we started receiving cancellations. To solve this problem, we sat down with Mercedes, and she devised a consignment plan with all the stores that were canceling. With this plan, the stores take the product anyway with no risk. It worked, and each of the stores sold out of the product.

Currently, *Bohden James* is sold in boutiques nationwide and in Japan, South America, and Canada. The men's fashion trade publication *Defining Men's Fashion* stated that we were "The New Generation of Sophistication," and the vice president of Universal Gear said, "Bohden James is a lifestyle brand that hangs exceptionally next to Hugo Boss, D&G, Ted Baker, and many other high-end exclusive brands while still having its own identity in the booming men's business." Without the help of mentors, our success would have not been a reality.

People that are successful in all industries want to help new and young business owners succeed. I didn't know anything about the clothing industry until I worked with one of my mentors who still helps me to this day toward achieving my goals. One of the biggest lessons I learned in business is that there is no "get rich quick" scheme to make money. In life you have to be passionate in what you do in order to make yourself successful. Once you are a success at what you do, the money will come. Originally, I went into my business with a connection rather than a passion, but I realized that attitude did not work out for me. Then, I developed a passion for the business. That attitude is something I learned from experience, and I learned from my father who is passionate and successful every day because he loves what he does.

I believe everyone should try to find three mentors in life. A personal mentor, an educational mentor, and a business mentor. They will all help with aspects of experience that we can learn from and improve our lives everyday. One of my educational mentors is my college professor John Hughes. He is someone I feel comfortable going to talk to about anything regarding business, education, or even my personal life. He has helped me make the right decisions throughout school and in my personal life.

I happen to be extremely lucky to have access to many mentors that are willing to help me along with anything I want to accomplish. In life everyone should do three things: Don't be afraid to ask for help, be honest, and love what you do. I didn't start to see success until I learned how to accomplish these things.

Tyler Olson

With a passion for providing enjoyable learning experiences for himself and others, Tyler hopes that his current business, ***Help-MeTy.com,*** is the precursor of many business ventures. At an early age, Tyler discovered that he learns best in a competitive environment where he is forced to act upon the lessons that he has learned. Upon completing a class in the foundations of entrepreneurship at the University of St. Thomas in the spring of 2006, Tyler decided to test his ideas in the marketplace. Being interested in technology, he started a computer support and web design business, ***HelpMeTy.com.*** The business was first based in his dorm room. However, one day Tyler walked into his 11' x 14' dorm only to find three of his technicians working on ten different computers. Immediately, he started his search for an office and within a few weeks moved his operations. Only a year later, the "world headquarters" of **HelpMeTy.com** grew from its initial office of 250 square feet to one of over 1,000 square feet. Presently, with his web design business, **HelpMeTy.com,** expanding, Tyler is continually motivated to create various challenges and learning experiences. Tyler looks forward to his most recent venture capital initiatives.

I discovered at an early age that I learn by doing. In attempting to learn to do many things well, I have become an entrepreneur. I start businesses to test my ideas and to force myself to learn more, and to learn faster. For me, entrepreneurship is the art of creating outlets that drive this symbiotic cycle of learning, doing, and learning more. One of the most important strategies of this art is to surround myself with those who can teach me, those who are better than me in many areas. If I am to achieve my goals, I need to soak in their experience and guidance. I was twelve years old when the light of entrepreneurship beamed into my life. While at my grandparents' cabin, the lady next door came over and asked if there were a teenager who could fix her computer. Being an extrovert, I raised my hand and said, "Well, I am not a teenager yet, but I would love to fix your computer." Sure enough, I did, and she asked what she owed me. Having no idea what to say next, I asked for what I was craving at that moment, brownies. That experience inspired a craving for starting my own businesses. Since that day, I have started about a dozen businesses ranging from lawn mowing, to selling cardboard boxes during college move-out day, to my current business, *HelpMeTy.com.*

Through my youth, my parents provided a vision of a lifestyle worth pursuing. The ability, someday, to not have to worry at all about money, to take weeks off of work if the family is in need, to do whatever I want, and to have whatever I want. Additionally, they taught me to believe in myself. They consistently reminded me that I was capable of whatever I wanted. As I look back upon my life, my parents' entire lives seem to be devoted to helping me achieve this vision for myself.

Being a young entrepreneur is hard. We are expected to be experts at managing payroll, taxes, liabilities, risks, finances, marketing, offices, sales, clients, customer service, public relations, and, most importantly, people. For many young entrepreneurs, we have never taken classes in the majority of these subjects. Succeeding at entrepreneurship takes a mind that can soak in incredible amounts of information on every subject quickly. However, more importantly, it requires a mind that is not only willing to listen to others, but also is open to receive another's knowledge and wisdom.

My life has consisted of a constant stream of mentors. Being someone who thrives on constantly learning more and at a faster rate than those around me, I learn as much as I can as quickly as I can from those who I believe are doing better than I am. Since first grade when I began my education in accelerated classes, I always wanted to be in the top of my class. I remember in sixth grade, we had a "top ten fastest typists" board. There were several of us constantly striving for the top position. Similarly, when I started to get into multiplayer video games, I would pick one or two games and understand the inner workings of that game better than anybody else, so I would always win.

None of this may sound like it has to do with mentors. However, I see mentors in all of the above situations. I wanted to learn from those who were doing a better job than me at everything. I would study with the top math students, top debaters, and top science students in the school. Many of these students I would classify as mentors of mine. While at the University of St. Thomas, again, I wanted to be ahead of the pack, so I associated as much as possible with people already doing businesses. I joined BizLounge, a twin cities entrepreneurship organization, to learn from other entrepreneurs. Because I had just recently started my business, I saw these members as mentors. Within a couple of months, I was asked to be on the board, and I jumped on the opportunity. The BizLounge Board became mentors of mine as I struggled with early entrepreneurial issues, and they helped me get off of the ground. On numerous occasions, they provided financial, legal, and marketing insight. As my business grew, fellow members of BizLounge and my professors informed me of the Entrepreneurs' Organization, the Accelerator program, and GSEA. Of course, these opportunities excited me, and I jumped on board as soon as I could.

Now that I look back, many of my best memories from the last twelve months have been related to these programs. It excites me to be able to anticipate all of the opportunities and learning experiences that await me within this program.

During the Global Student Entrepreneur Award competition, I took every opportunity I could to talk with the other competitors and judges. I knew that my business was doing less in revenue than most of the businesses owned by the people at the competition. However, I was eager to grow and to learn. I quickly learned how important it is to simply believe that you can triple the size of your business in one year and to go for it. Even though my business had grown about 500% from the year before, I sincerely did not believe it would be able to keep that up much longer. Fortunately, this room of people was able to re-inspire me to find new ways to grow larger and faster. I have kept the tripling effect in my mind since that event, and we are on pace to do that this year. I believe it is possible to achieve that momentum next year as well.

When I participated as an international finalist in the Global Student Entrepreneur Awards, I was amazed at the number of students with businesses doing more than one million dollars in sales. How many college students would you trust with a budget of more than a million dollars? Hearing the stories of these young entrepreneurs, including one from a nineteen year old doing three million in sales, inspired me. In many respects, I consider them mentors because they freely shared ideas that fundamentally shifted how I look at the potential of business and ignited a fire within me to shoot yet higher than I previously thought was possible. While growing my business, I have found few things to be as beneficial as simply being around people who have a larger vision and are better at acting upon that vision.

While at the competition, many Entrepreneur Organization members encouraged me to meet one of the judges, Shane Erickson, who is from my local area. After my conversations with Shane and others, I knew that I needed to join the Accelerator program and have an EO mentor. Within a few months, I attended my first Accelerator event and chose to have Shane as my mentor. Shane has helped me to understand entrepreneurship from an entirely new angle. As a serial entrepreneur, investor, and business consultant, he opens my eyes to new realities of business that I did not know existed. When bouncing ideas off of him, his responses take us in directions that showcase a potential ten times greater than I previously thought possible. Additionally, his relationship to his business inspires and motivates me. At a recent Accelerator conference, the speaker asked the question, "Is there anybody in this room who could leave their business for a month starting today and feel comfortable?" Shane was the only person in the room who raised his hand. His ability to transition his business to one that no longer requires his mind and skills is a part of the great entrepreneurial dream that I aspire to reach someday. In recent months, Shane and I have been working through a new business idea. His guidance, advice, and encouragement are priceless. There is nothing like talking with an entrepreneur you greatly respect and have him say, "I believe you will have a very successful business someday, and I would like to invest in you." I heard those words of encouragement from Shane.

Many entrepreneurs struggle internally with arrogance. I am no exception. We need to be leaders; we need to understand how everything works; we need to be great at many roles, and many of us naturally believe that we are the most important or the best person in the company. Still, what simultaneously drives our business forward and keeps us humble is the awareness that there are always people better at what we do than we are. It is that realization that motivates us. Even in the moment when we have mastered what we set out to accomplish, we are envisioning the next goals we want to achieve. These goals are inevitably more challenging and more exciting, requiring an ever greater use of mentorship. This is the spirit of being an entrepreneur.

Brendan Ciecko

Brendan Ciecko, 20, is the founder and CEO of *Ten Minute Media*, a driving force in the realm of interactive media and creative marketing. At the age of twelve, Ciecko started producing websites for emerging rock bands. He quickly transformed his talents into a thriving business. Since its official establishment in 2003, *Ten Minute Media* has acquired an impressive and flourishing list of major clients: Warner Brothers, Universal, Sony BMG, RCA, Capitol Records as well as Fortune 500 giants, Clear Channel and MassMutual.

With such an impressive resume, Ciecko has gained the attention of the national press. In 2007, *Ten Minute Media* received *PC Magazine*'s Small Business Award for innovative use of technology. In addition, in its article "Making It Big," *Entrepreneur Magazine* featured Ciecko's company and its success. Behind Ciecko's business persona exists his own artistic and musical essence. It is in this experience that Ciecko takes most pride, especially having worked with music icons Mick Jagger, Natalie Cole, and Bob Seger. In his spare time, Ciecko is a leader in the efforts to revitalize historic downtown Holyoke, a post-industrial city in Massachusetts.

There I was running from 8th Ave. to Park Ave. on the busy streets of Manhattan. Since I had no cash in my pocket, catching a cab was not an option. My only mode of transportation was my own two feet. Why was I running in such a hurry? Well, I was approaching an opportunity of a lifetime, and I was not about to be late, not even by a second. In just a few minutes, I was to meet with Mick Jagger of The Rolling Stones. The way that I was dodging taxis, baby carriages, and all pedestrians in my path, my sprint could have easily been a Nike™ commercial. As I arrived at my destination, I checked my watch and saw that I had two minutes to spare. Gathering my thoughts, I asked myself, "Is this what being an entrepreneur is all about? How did I make it to this point?"

Since a young age, I have been fascinated and intrigued by technology, music, and design. When I was not playing guitar in my punk rock band, I was glued to my computer screen learning anything and everything I could about how the internet worked. I saw the web as a very powerful tool that put everything at my finger tips. I wanted to learn how to create websites, and I taught myself the ins and outs of countless programs. By the age of twelve, I started producing websites for rock bands, and I quickly turned this hobby of mine into a business. As my capabilities and knowledge evolved, so did my venture.

My regular weapon of choice in this business: the keys. I mean, keyboard...the one attached to your personal computer. That may sound a bit geeky, which it is, but it's the honest truth. I even wear the glasses to prove it. My passion for design and technology became the vehicle that delivered me through the trenches of both business and the music industry.

In 2003, I founded *Ten Minute Media* to take my skills to the next level and to offer my clients creative design and innovative marketing. Our initial focus was to specialize in website development in the music and entertainment industry. Currently, our list of clientele includes Clear Channel, Warner Brothers, Capitol Music, Sony BMG, Universal, along with many other companies across the board. My portfolio is filled with websites for legends such as Mick Jagger, Natalie Cole, and Bob Seger; interactive marketing tools for Eric Clapton, Josh Groban, and Lily Allen; and design work for chart-toppers, System of a Down and One Republic. In the past year, we have seen a great increase in demand for our services outside of our niche, the music market.

Consequently, to challenge their industry's status quo, we have started to offer corporations a web presence that is unique and exciting.

Until about a year ago, I had been operating my business relying on only my own intuition. I had no one to call upon in times of trials and tribulations. Reading books and attending seminars on business could only take me a short distance. At the rapid rate that my business was advancing, I needed someone with extensive experience to help with these business "growing pains." I needed a living, breathing mentor, so I began my search.

In May of 2007, I went to Boston to compete in the Global Student Entrepreneur Awards (GSEA) regional finals. At the time, I was a first-year student at a liberal, laissez-faire college in Amherst, MA. I felt as though I had been living under a rock. While in Boston, I had the task of presenting my company to the esteemed members of the Entrepreneurs Organization (EO). The panel of judges in Boston overflowed with suggestions, advice and perspective that I had previously never encountered. I saw this experience as a great opportunity to find a mentor, and it seemed that the EO members saw this as a chance to help guide a young entrepreneur. In the weeks that followed, I met with a few of these EO members, and soon after, I found the three individuals that best understood my vision and could help me strengthen my business.

Having mentors that are successful in various fields, other than my own, provides me with an unbiased and dynamic perspective. This view also creates a healthy and advantageous balance from which a young entrepreneur learns. After coming to these conclusions, I was led to a mentor from my own surrounding area of Springfield, MA. Although our businesses are very different, this difference is not important. What is important is that we share the same values. His experience in the socially responsible sector has inspired me to be an entrepreneur who is conscious of more than just balance sheets and profit margins. This being said, I have a few mentors with extremely diverse backgrounds. My adviser from Springfield, MA, is on the forefront of social responsibility and ethical business; whereas, one of my EO mentors is on the cutting-edge of technology and marketing strategy—this formula strikes an equilibrium that is beneficial to me.

For me, a mentor is not someone who I need contact on a regular basis or who knows my every move. He or she is someone I can call upon anytime and receive honest and objective advice.

My own advice to young entrepreneurs is: know why you're in business. I've heard this numerous times, but its truth is timeless. Secondly, align your business with your missions, values and goals. Ask yourself why you are in business. Are you in business just to make money, offer high-quality services, fill a void, shake up the marketplace? Knowing why you do what you do will help you navigate through times of uncertainty. During those times, you can always resort to your founding principles. Going about your business in this way, you'll feel happier and more fulfilled. Find mentors early in your entrepreneurial venture. Their knowledge and honest concern will help guide you in the right direction. *Ten Minute Media* has a long way to go, and there is no question that mentorship will continue to accelerate that process.

Seeing the positive impact that mentoring has had on me and my business, I've started to mentor young entrepreneurs from the inner cities of the greater Springfield area. This allows me to share the knowledge that I have gained from some of the best business people I know. Since my mentors helped me, I believe that it is my duty to do the same for others and connect with my community.

It is astounding to think about how becoming an entrepreneur changed my life. As I worked on websites from my bedroom when I was twelve years old, I never once imagined that this interest of mine would open numerous doors to a bright future. The truth is that anyone who has drive and dedication, no matter their background, social or economic status, has the ability to become a successful entrepreneur. It is endearing to read stories about people from all over the world, of all ages, races, and ethnicities, finding their inner passion or interest and turning that into an enterprise that can single-handedly change their life in a positive way and impact the people around them. Entrepreneurship is an ode to freedom and creativity. Don't get me wrong, there are many challenges in starting your own business—there are tremendous responsibilities and much personal sacrifice, but being an entrepreneur is one of the most rewarding endeavors in life. It's gratifying to know that my creations are being viewed all around the world and to realize that I got to this point through pure diligence and determination.

Entrepreneurship is one of life's great equalizers. In a world of global inequality, the concept of people going from rags to riches gives us hope that we are capable of creating something extraordinary out of nothing.

As you finish reading my last sentence, I recommend that you put down this book and start the business that's been on your mind. Put your ideas to good use. Put down this book and get going!

William Fikhman

William Fikhman was born with an entrepreneurial spirit. At the young age of ten, after making stress balls for a class activity, Fikhman capitalized on the opportunity and began manufacturing stress balls at home. He then proceeded to sell these home-made stress balls to family and friends for one dollar each. His entrepreneurial spirit continued to drive William. At twelve, he started a dog-walking service. He soon hired two employees to work for him while he managed the client relationships and revenue collections. At sixteen, William broadened his ambitions, and he began selling artwork at a local art gallery. Here, he learned and refined his unique style of selling. In December 2004, at the age of nineteen, Fikhman became one of the first and youngest owners of an *iSold It* franchise, a drop-off store concept that helps people sell their items on eBay. In just four months after his first store's opening, William

Fikhman raised an additional $150,000 in capital and went on to open his second location in 2005. Sales steadily grew, and in 2006, sales topped one million dollars. This success prompted *Entrepreneur's Start Up* magazine to feature Fikhman as one of "7 Entrepreneurs Who've Hit It Big before Their 25th Birthdays."

Fikhman has continued to aggressively expand and cultivate his business. In 2007, he opened sales to countries beyond the United States. Presently, Fikhman's company sells to China, the United Kingdom, Australia and Canada. He also plans to expand *iSold It* beyond eBay to become the connection between the online and physical worlds. In the coming months, William Fikhman will increase his business by selling products across numerous online platforms such as Amazon, Shop.com, uBid and other e-commerce channels.

As an entrepreneur, Fikhman continues to develop. With a deep passion for learning, Fikhman is completing his senior year at California State University, Northridge, where he is majoring in accounting and business. His academic efforts have been recognized with William's being awarded Dean's List Honors for five consecutive semesters. William approaches his academic environment as he does his business endeavors...with total dedication. He devotes a large portion of his time to student organizations including Accounting Association, Beta Alpha Psi, Alpha Epsilon Pi and the Business Honors Association.

Working the Media Room

On December 17, 2007, at 6:30 PM on a Monday night, on prime time TV my business, *iSold It,* was featured. Why? One month prior, we were approached by a person who had worked as the personal assistant to entertainer Britney Spears. Through the course of their relationship, Britney's assistant became her friend, and, as friends sometimes do, started to share wardrobes. The assistant ended up with a few dresses, a jacket and a red dress—not just any red dress, but the red dress worn by Britney Spears on the day that Britney forgot to wear underwear...and the world found out. Who doesn't know about that episode in Britney news history?

Knowing about the "fate" of the red dress, I inform the public relations at TMZ. They love the story and run it. In the meantime, I continue to check the sales on eBay: Britney outfit...twenty-three watchers. No big change, just normal. After lunch, I check eBay again, as always. Britney outfit... sixty-nine watchers; my experience tells me, "WHOAH! What happened?" Keeping track of the dress's progress, I logon to TMZ.com. On its front page for the world to see was the story of the Britney Red Dress and our store. With that little bit of exposure, we broke the PR barrier. The surge that experience gave to me was amazing.

Quickly, my mind begins to plot the next move and the move after that, and maybe, some alternatives. Move one is to answer the questions, "How do we keep this attention?" Or as Eminem would say, "What if you had just one shot, one opportunity? What would you do?" My immediate next step is to secure more inventory. I call my brother Mike who is also my assistant, and we secure more inventory. After we inform TMZ, we plan a publicity shoot in our store.

The TMZ cameraman shows up at the store at 9:00 AM Friday to film the next week's footage. The story airs Monday night. The two minute clip shows our storefront, informs people of the difficulty of selling on eBay, and promotes my business, *iSold It*, as the option chosen by the celebrities, even Britney Spears. The event, particularly the PR exposure, was perfect. I couldn't have asked for anything more. I came home late the night the TV segment aired, and I started to think about what I learned from these events and people; what I was doing, and, most importantly, why do I think the way that I think? The lesson I learned is not all about PR. It is entirely about seeing opportunity, especially the opportunity for self-improvement through learning. This realization helped me to prepare for my next step, competition.

Although I had very limited exposure or experience in PR, I carefully and proudly prepared my presentation for the *2007 Global Student Entrepreneur Awards*. Later, at the competition, I learned how other contestants and entrepreneurs very similar to myself had advanced in PR; no doubt, they were better! I spent hours talking to all of them about what worked and what didn't work, what difficulties they experienced, how they overcame those difficulties, and how they created, built, envisoned.

I didn't win the competition, but I came home a winner. I went to the competition desiring to win, thinking I had a realistic chance to win. However, after seeing and talking to other contestants, it was clear I would not win. Although my experience had me far ahead of some; there were others who were much more experienced, who had overcome many more challenges, and who had contributed more significantly. In retrospect, preparing my presentation for this competition helped me organize my thoughts and put my business plans on paper. Being surrounded by other smart and successful people gave me the opportunity to absorb valuable knowledge. It also gave me a most important gift, inspiration.

I urge you, entrepreneur, to see the opportunity in every situation, especially in those situations that do not go your way. Make that negative go your way. Make it work for YOU. And, if you can't get what you want out of something, get something else out of it to hold you over, because from every experience you will get what you really, really want and what you really, really need. Go, forward, full forward!

Marcel Berger

From an early age, Marcel Berger had "hands on" experience in the operations and management of major events and worked in management roles in the hospitality and arts industries in Australia, and in other countries abroad. These skills, along with a life-long commitment to fitness, have helped drive Marcel Berger's current business, **Get a Life...Health Management.**

At the tender age of seventeen, Marcel successfully established and managed a small café in Melbourne, Australia. During his last years of formal education, Marcel continued to dabble in small business ventures. Marcel's entrepreneurial fires continued to burn until he finally embarked on a life-changing trip to London— where he would establish and manage a successful cocktail bar in Camden Town. The experiences Marcel gleaned through these ventures guided his present business success.

Get a Life... is a preventative health management company
offering innovative solutions to corporate organizations and busy
individuals. Since its inception in 2004, *Get a Life...* has worked
with over twenty-five of Australia's leading organizations and
helped over 6,500 Australians live healthier lives.

Marcel has been a tireless supporter of community organizations such as Murdoch Children's Research Institute, HeartKids
Victoria and 3MBS Classically Melbourne.

Over the past four years, I have been guided through
my never-ending development as an entrepreneur.
I am honored to have been mentored by CEOs, professors,
media experts and successful business people. Through them,
I have learned a great deal about how to create and run a successful business, find the necessary drive and motivation when
the chips are down, and how to be ethical and honorable, not
only in business, but also in life.

To show how mentors have become an invaluable part of
my career and life in general, I will start at the beginning....

My current business, *Get a Life...Health Management (Get
a Life...)* spawned from a university project in early 2004. At
RMIT Entrepreneurship in Australia, we undertake an exer-
cise in our first year whereby each of the seventy students pres-

ents to the class three proposals of business concepts. In class, the students were paired up and asked to decide which of the concepts will prove most viable in the real world. This process was repeated until there were ten business concepts remaining. *Get a Life* was one of these concepts.

Seven bright-eyed students were brought together with one goal in mind: to make *Get a Life...* a reality. Our first hurdle was the initial setup of the corporate structure through which *Get a Life...* would operate. We were all first-year entrepreneurship majors, but we had never set up a business before. To help us through this period, I took advantage of the skill, expertise and mentorship of two of my lecturers, Colin Dunn, the entrepreneurship coordinator at RMIT, and David Southwick, our resident serial entrepreneur, political candidate and all-round successful businessman. Their doors are always open, and their assistance invaluable.

You are probably saying to yourselves that being top entrepreneurship students we must have known what to do to make an idea into a reality, and, to a point, you would be right. What we did not know, however, was the situations that are not taught in books, the specifics that only trial and error and experience teach. This is where Colin and David really added value; they had been there; they had their failures and ultimately succeeded. They provided the advice we needed to commercialize our venture and bring our dreams to fruition. Even though my contact with these two mentors has been reduced since the initial setup of *Get a Life...*, I know I can always call upon them if I need any advice. This sense of security is one of the major benefits of mentorship.

After the project was no longer assessable, four of the original seven students dropped off, leaving three of us who were committed to making *Get a Life...* commercially viable. This decision was supported by my mentors.

All of the months of strategic planning paid off, and on the morning of February 10, 2005, *Get a Life...* received its first phone call which resulted in our first sale, and before we knew it, we were in business. Sales picked up over the next few months, and by June 2005, *Get a Life...* was generating modest revenues of over $2000 a month.

It was at this time that I received the most beneficial piece of advice yet, and it came from the least likely source, my mother, Lin Bender. Her suggestion was to establish a hand-picked advisory group of mentors to assist in the strategic development of *Get a Life...* That suggestion started a chain of events that has led *Get a Life...* to its current status as a national health provider, and that advice assisted in our global expansion through our online media arm.

The Approach

I knew that *Get a Life...* had great potential, and we were at the critical stage in the establishment of any business. At this stage it is easier to give up and get a job than it is to keep going. We were cash-strapped, had limited manpower and resources and realized that if *Get a Life...* were going to take off, we needed to think laterally. How were we going to grow *Get a Life...* into a viable, profitable and successful business that could help busy people all over the world live healthier lifestyles?

The strategy for establishing the advisory group sounded easy, but the challenge was to identify precisely which skills were required, to identify the best people who had these skills, and to work out how to get to them. I had to ask these individuals to join an advisory group which required a commitment of a meeting once a month with no remuneration. Sounds simple, right?

Well, as many twenty-three-year-olds who have just gone out and started a business not knowing what they got themselves into, I was petrified at the prospect of approaching these leading business people, and I expected them to dismiss me as they do junk emails.

As always, my mother's advice was right. Start with the most influential target and work out how to get to them through your existing network—the rest falls into place. My group of handpicked business leaders not only agreed to my proposal, but they also embraced the opportunity to help me grow *Get a Life...* from a small business into a national organization.

My first target was Steve Harris, who at the time was the CEO of the Melbourne Football Club, the oldest football club in the world and Australia's equivalent to the New York Jets. Steve was also the former editor-in-chief of Melbourne's two leading newspapers, *The Age* and *The Herald Sun*. Approaching Steve was daunting; however, I knew that if I could communicate my passion and vision for the business, he would jump on board, and that is exactly what he did.

Apart from his media experience, Steve brought with him valuable corporate knowledge, and his familiarity of corporate bureaucracy was invaluable in navigating our approach to large organizations. Even though he would not like me saying this, Steve also brought wisdom to the table. Since the rest of my mentors are younger, I believe it is important to have at least one mentor who has been around the block and brings years of experience to the table.

Above all, the greatest value Steve brought was his network, and I am forever grateful for the number of doors that

Steve opened for me and for the people I have been introduced to. My first meeting with Steve introduced me to my future chairman, friend and mentor, Adam Jacoby. I was in the Melbourne Football Club boardroom chatting with Steve about a potential university placement at the club, and Steve had the foresight to invite Adam to join us.

While we were all chatting about a potential project for me to work on for my university assignment, Steve asked me to talk about my business, *Get a Life...* and so I did. We had not realized that three hours later we had spoken about a potential project for only fifteen minutes; the rest was all about *Get a Life...*

While explaining the ins and outs of *Get a Life...*, Adam mentioned that he too had a similar business ten years prior which was ahead of its time. He saw an opportunity to develop the business into the world's leading action sports management firm, IMS Sports. This was the first time that I had met someone who shared my vision and could see eye to eye with me. Adam and I immediately bonded; he joined the advisory group and, with Steve's blessing, took on the role of chairman. The relationship with Adam seemed to click from day one. He had worked in the arts and sports sector; he is passionate about great ideas, innovation and creative thinking, and he is one of the most intelligent and inspiring people I know. Now, three years later, I am even more impressed with Adam's compassion, intelligence, enthusiasm and values, all of which he has taught to me.

My group of mentors was almost complete. I had the experience of Steve Harris, the creativity and drive of Adam Jacoby, and the logic and values of my mother. Now, I needed someone who was a leader in health.

I found exactly who I was looking for one morning while attending a networking event. My business partner and I had been given tickets to a large networking event (that I normally hate) and decided that we may as well go along and take advantage of a free breakfast. When we arrived, we found that the keynote speaker was Sherry Strong, a little lady with a big personality who also happened to be an internationally acclaimed chef and energy coach and the former state chair of Nutrition Australia. I turned to Matt and said, "We must have her in the advisory group." Matt, of course, agreed.

At the end of the event, I picked up enough courage to push through the crowd and speak with Sherry. I explained *Get a Life...* and what we were trying to do and invited Sherry to meet with us at our office to talk about the health issues that confront corporate Australia. To my surprise, Sherry agreed to meet the following week; that meeting resulted in her agreement to join the advisory group.

I was now surrounded with a CEO, a successful entrepreneur and a highly respected health expert along with my "bank of mentors" who have always remained on call. We were now ready to take the business to the next level. As I now look back, I understand the value of the strategic advice that this "dream team" provided. I did all the work, but they encouraged, made me believe in myself, as I mentioned earlier, opened doors and—above all—stopped me from giving up.

A Helping Hand

Over the past three years my mentoring group has helped me through the tough times, celebrated the good times and supported my decisions no matter how big or small. The security of knowing that I can call upon any of my many mentors gives me the confidence to push the boundaries in business and life. Being entrepreneurial is difficult. It involves breaking new ground, having a vision for taking new pathways, convincing others to follow your vision, and, then, having the responsibility to turn that vision into a reality. Having a group of like-minded people around you makes all the difference. It provides a safety net, and I am forever grateful to my mentors for providing me with this security.

There are so many practical instances when my advisory group made all the difference. A perfect example happened about a year ago when we had a major potential deal with a major corporate rewards company. We had worked hard to get in front of the CEO and propose our organization for a strategic partnership; however, we were two twenty-somethings with a small business trying to negotiate with a large national organization. We were through the first stage of the negotiation, and I still remember being terrified of going to the next level with their senior people. My chairman, Adam Jacoby, had introduced a new advisor to the group, James Newman, New Business Director for Australia's largest media company, Fairfax. Adam and James sat down with Matt and me to help devise a strategy, develop a draft agreement, and prepare us for the meeting. This was a great help, but we were still nervous. Empathizing with our position, James put up his hand to join the negotiation as a support. Our confidence soared by having James there. We knew that he would jump in where necessary and reiterate our main points in a more concise way, and this helped us progress further with the deal.

Another of my mentors, who I never thought would become such a close friend, is one of my old lecturers, Peter Christo. Peter and I worked closely when he was in need of a junior consultant on one of his projects. I ended up working

with Peter for twelve months as his junior, and he taught me
the processes involved in strategic business consulting. Peter
has been invaluable over the years; however, I remember
when I was very down about *Get a Life...* We were really struggling, and I was very close to shutting up shop, winding up the
business and going to work full time. This, of course, would
have been a much easier option. Peter would not have a bar
of it. He sat me down over a coffee and told me the stories of
how he had been in similar positions, hugging the toilet bowl
at night while not knowing how he was going to pay his staff
in the morning. Hearing someone I respect talk about going
through the same scenario helped give me the confidence to
push through the situation. We did get through, picked up
sales and since then have been doubling our revenues.

Reflecting on the past four years, I realize the importance
of surrounding yourself with a group of like-minded individuals who you can bounce off, learn from and most importantly,
use as a support structure. I am fortunate to have a group of
mentors who helped make me believe that I had it in me.

A successful mentorship is a relationship that extends
beyond the parameters of the project. In every instance, the
relationship was built on mutual respect and developed into
friendship. When I think of the influences all of my mentors
have had on me, I'm struck most by their ability to deconstruct

what looks like a negative scenario and create a positive one. This has been imprinted into my psyche by a phrase told to me by my most inspirational mentor, my mother, and I would like to leave you with this same phrase.

"There is no such thing as a problem, only an opportunity."

Jeff Livney

Jeff founded *Livney+Partners,* formerly *Piko Zoom,* in September 2003, and continues to manage its growth and expansion. After noticing a disconnect between many web design firms and the typical entrepreneur or small organization client, Jeff decided that there must be an easier, less traditional means of creating effective marketing campaigns. With that goal in mind, and bypassing the more strategic messaging and marketing campaigns, Jeff founded his company on a client-centric foundation. He guides the company by values that establish long-term relationships with clients, and his company approaches each campaign as though that campaign were his company's own.

This approach did not go unrecognized. In 2006, Jeff was named the Texas Youth Entrepreneur of the Year by Texas Christian University. In addition, in March 2006, Jeff was featured on the cover of the *Houston Business Journal,* and Jeff's company,

Livney+Partners was named "One of Houston's Largest Website

Development Firms" by the *Houston Business Journal.* Jeff is also

involved in the Dallas/Fort Worth and Houston communities; he is

a judge for the Fort Worth Chamber of Commerce's "Rising Star"

Small Business of the Year competition, and he is an active member

in Accelerator, a Houston Entrepreneurs' Organization program,

as well as in other associations and philanthropic groups.

I am often questioned about how a high school kid finds his way into marketing. I have lost count of how many times I have been told, "I've heard of kids starting lawn services and fix-it type companies… but a marketing firm?" After the obligatory "I'm kind of a big deal" quip, my usual response has something to do with persistence, mentorship, and a Texas-sized serving of luck.

Oddly enough, my career in marketing all started with a dream of being an attorney. Coming from a family with attorneys, being an attorney was the only career that a kid could dream. I wanted to be Alan Shore, not Judge Judy (you have to have the right visual, or this story holds no relevance.) So, being the eager and naïve high school sophomore that I was,

I figured I would go intern in a law office. Sure, law offices generally take law school interns, maybe college interns, but I figured that I was just as smart as the rest of them. And... I wanted to get paid too.

That was the plan. Turns out, law firms don't really want or even consider having high school students on staff. I was not deterred. Off to California I went to intern in my aunt's law office. Like many adults, my aunt assumed that all young people know everything about computers and the Internet and websites, so my project was to build a website for the firm. In reality, I knew very little about technology except for how to Google. However, I did have a friend back home in Texas who had built some websites, so I subcontracted the project to him and spent my time enjoying the California summers. "And thus an entrepreneur was born," they say.

After we launched the website for the law firm, I started receiving calls from people who saw the website or heard about it from my family. I started getting calls requesting that I design different types of website projects, and I found free-lancers online to do them for me. If a client needed a logo, too, I'd find someone to do that. And pretty soon, I was doing all sorts of projects, from websites to logos to direct mail to print advertising. A big break happened when my photojournalism teacher mentioned my company to her husband, who was looking to hire a firm to build a website for his new company. This little project ended up being much bigger.

John Landsbaum hired me to build a small website for a new sales and marketing firm he was starting with a colleague. John, a former board member and VP at Enterprise Rent-a-Car, ended up having an incredible impact on the growth of my fledging business. Through his national network of very successful business owners, I was soon doing projects for all sorts of clients, who would in turn refer other clients, and, soon, word was spreading faster than a "grassfire with a tailwind." For a high school student, the growth was more than exciting. While my friends were begging their parents to tap into their trust funds, I was earning my own money, much more than a teenager who was earning only minimum wage.

Soon, John Landsbaum introduced me to a good friend of his, David Keilson, who owned a car dealership. David was one of the youngest dealership owners at the time and loved the idea of youth entrepreneurship. Their guidance, support, and referrals led to some big projects. We were doing direct mail campaigns for JPMorgan Chase, branding for a real estate company, print design for Marriott Hotels and so on.

Another opportunity came when my high school counselor heard about a scholarship for high school students who own businesses in Texas, and I submitted an application. A couple of months later, twenty-five or so finalists from around the state convened for workshops and interviews at the Neeley Entrepreneurship Center at Texas Christian University in Fort Worth, where I was named the grand prize winner (and awarded $10,000).

To recognize this honor, one of my public relations clients offered to write a release and send it out in exchange for some services. That is when I really learned how one little action can make a big impact. I forwarded the press release to the editor of the *Houston Business Journal* by email. A couple days later, the journal sent out a photographer to take some pictures of me, and I was interviewed on the phone. I was anticipating some small article buried somewhere in the paper.

However, when the issue was published, one of my biggest clients at the time, the owner of the real estate company, who I had never personally met, called me. "You little shit. I have socks older than you. I'm reading this article on the cover of *HBJ*... I thought you were thirty-five or something." That phone call will always stick with me.

At that point, numerous calls followed. Although the *HBJ* article and other publications did not lead to many solid leads, they did solidify (and continue to do so) prospects at the time.

This awareness is something I always tell people: "Don't expect the publicity to propel your business overnight; it's more of a stepping stone when prospects find out you have been in *The Business Journal,* the local paper and on radio." This is when mentorship became a much more integral role in the growth of the company. Up until this point, the best way to describe the company would be that it was like a mutt—it could be anything, but nobody knows exactly what. There was no solid infrastructure, brand, or plans for the future.

Mentorship propelled the company into something moldable. When I went to college, the invaluable resources at the Neeley Entrepreneurship Center at TCU have been very integral to scaling the company. David Minor, Ash Huzenlaub and Brad Hancock, director, board of advisor member and assistant director, respectively, of the Neeley Entrepreneurship Center have helped me form a solid foundation for growth.

One of the biggest parts of having mentors for me has been the ability to utilize their networks. As longstanding and successful members of the business community, each of these men has a unique network of people and organizations that provide sound advice and services. It is their ideas, and often criticisms, which help me establish relationships and scale the business.

Of course, the first step of the entrepreneur's journey is to select mentors that are a good fit for your needs. There are plenty of successful individuals that love to help young entrepreneurs get started. Mentoring gives many people a sense of giving back to the community. Others just do it for their love of entrepreneurship. Regardless of their motives, there are plenty of viable candidates for mentors, but you should be careful when establishing that relationship.

An article in *The New York Times* addresses this point perfectly. Marci Alboher's "Advice on Mentors, From One of Mine" (Sept. 25, 2007) offers a great guide for the steps to take. Her third tip really drives my point home: Approach the first meeting with restraint. Do not ask for favors. Be humble, but approach with praise about how impressed you are with their success, and how you aspire to be in their place one day. One thing to keep in mind, and forgive me for the stereotype, is that most entrepreneurs are very impressed with themselves. Honestly, they should be. They build wealth for themselves, their employees and better the community. For the most part, I have found that a character trait of most entrepreneurs is that they love telling their story. They often just love their voice. So, let them do a lot of the talking. Ask to hear their story, their life lessons and experiences and anecdotes. Make the first meeting about them, and you'll be surprised how quickly future meetings can become about you, your ideas and business aspirations.

Zach Vruwink

Zach Vruwink is a true entrepreneur at heart. Vruwink was born in a small central Wisconsin community, and he understands the value of hard work, optimism and building lasting relationships. With that background, and with only $500, at the age of 15, Zach Vruwink founded **Zach's Computers LLC** . His company, a retail store located in the downtown area of Wisconsin Rapids, specializes in technology sales and service. To provide his customers with exceptional service, Zach created the "Zach's Advantage." This concept provides the customers with a non-threatening atmosphere and with the assistance that allows for a better understanding of technology. Owning a business was something Zach Vruwink always dreamed of doing, but due to the community's uncertain economy as well as his young age, owning his own business involved taking an incredible risk. However, the risk was rewarded. Vruwink is a recipient of the *Ernst & Young/Junior Achievement 2006 Young Entrepreneur of the Year Award*. Zach is also the winner of the *2007 Global Student Entrepreneur Award–Minnesota Region*. Currently, Zach is pursuing a degree in political science and economics. In addition to being a student, and a young entrepreneur, Zach is also actively involved in his community by contributing both his time and his financial support. Zach Vruwink owes his success to his belief in working together to create positive change, not only in business, but also in every endeavor that he pursues.

The journey of entrepreneurship comes with no specific road-map for success. Some individuals begin this journey earlier in life than others do; some achieve success on this journey earlier; others never will. Like all journeys, the journey of entrepreneurship does not guarantee a successful arrival at the destination. As a student entrepreneur who started a business while I was the age of 15, I would like to share my experience and some of the important lessons that I have learned thus far on my own journey.

Startup

As a child, I often wondered where I would be after high school; as a high school student, I wondered where I would be after college. I was always intrigued by business, how it operated and how it functioned in society. After I began my high school career, I became anxious to get a part-time job. However, because of economic uncertainty in my community, a result of the single largest employer being sold to a foreign buyer, I knew that prospects for my employment were slim. I did not want to work in a position that paid only minimum wage like most people my age, I had a yearning to be different. Consequently, I took a different path. During the fall of my freshman year, I was intrigued by technology, by how it worked, and by the endless opportunities that technology offered. I also had a talent for working with technology. As a result, I started providing on-demand computer services for family and friends, and this service soon grew. After earning a small amount of money and growing my network of customers, I decided to apply for a state seller's permit which would allow me to purchase products I needed at wholesale prices. In December of 2002, I received notification that my application had been approved. With that approval, Zach's Computers was born!

After a few months of continued growth, I continued to be amazed that my simple passion was continuing to fill a niche that until this time had not been filled. As summer vacation approached, I faced a difficult, but a positive decision. I had run out of space to continue to operate my business from my home. With this business growth, my dream of showcasing my products and services on a retail level turned into a drive and a possibility. On the bus ride home from school, I had noticed one of many for lease signs in a down-town storefront, and I noted the phone number. Too excited to wait, or think twice, I called the number and explained my interest in the location and asked for an appropriate time for me to tour the store. After finishing the conversation, I came to the realization that I, at the age of 15, had made my first business call! I was ecstatic! For the next few days, my mind raced on the thought of the unknown and the potential that existed.

In the coming days, I met with the woman representing the property management. I knew that the downtown location would be a perfect fit for my young business. I convinced my parents to support this idea. Because I was not yet 18, my mother agreed to negotiate the lease on a month-to-month status, under no obliga-tion to continue if things did not work. My dream was one step closer to reality! At that moment I had only $500 in my savings account . Of that savings, $400 went to pay my first month's rent, and the other $100 was committed to startup costs. With a planned "soft opening" in 4 weeks, an empty storefront and very little busi-ness experience, I had many activities and responsibilities to per-form. In the following few weeks, I moved the store fixtures that were acquired from a closing Kmart and filled them with the small inventory that I had in my basement. Further, with no capital sup-port from my parents, I knew that I had a tremendous amount of work ahead of me if I intended to pay my second month's rent. For-tunately, due to the support of the local media's writing of a front-page article about the business, I was able to gain the exposure needed to afford my second month's rent. Even to this day, people remember the front-page article titled "The Computer Kid." Even now, I am frequently asked whether or not I am the kid who started my business during high school. The three month summer break of selling and servicing computers soon passed, and I had yet another difficult decision to make. Would I close the doors and go back to start my sophomore year or attempt to do both? Regarding this question, there was little debate. I had to continue to provide the community with the services that I had provided for the past few months. This endeavor was not longer just a job for me, but it was a passion. Without hesitation, I began my sophomore year, in high school. I carried a full class schedule with no study halls. Each day after school, I was open for business.

Be Your Best Critique

Over the subsequent weeks, months, and years, trial and error became my best friend. I had no professional sales, marketing nor any management experience. Further, I had not reached out for mentoring support, I did however, become my best critique. Setting achievable goals while continuing to raise the bar higher was my indicator for success.

After three years of spreading myself very thin between school, my 'social life' and selling and servicing technology products, I decided to hire my first employee. It was a very difficult decision to make as I had previously done all of the jobs myself.

At this point it is important to note that I had no business administration experience or know-how aside from many hours of Internet research and asking many questions.

Be Responsive To Change

Change is inevitable. In my community, economic change has been ever present from the start of my business. As a result, I have been taught the importance of diversifying my product line as well as my services. In this way, I have been also successful in using the Internet as a vehicle for selling products to other markets. As an entrepreneur, it is also important to note that each day brings new opportunities as well as new challenges. These challenges will create the chance to strengthen and grow your business. For me, challenges presented resulting from change, have been my best teacher. It compelled me to rethink my attitude as well as redefine my optimism.

After five years in business, the greatest change has happened during the last year. Change that in numerous ways, has been essential to sustaining my success. I have focused on expanding and streamlining product lines and hiring additional staff. As a result, I have been successful in launching the much-anticipated Apple Authorized Reseller status, the Apple Authorized Service Center. In addition, I became an agent for a regional wireless cellular carrier. To the credit of much of my success, it is critical for me to mention the importance of reflecting on the past.

Reflect

In the spring of 2007, a member of the Entrepreneur's Organization (EO) encouraged me to apply for the *Global Student Entrepreneur Award*. This individual had become aware of my business in a press release issued by my school, the University Wisconsin-Stevens Point. I was shocked that an entrepreneur competition existed, and without much question, I started the application. In writing the application, I realized it was the first time I had reflected on my entrepreneurial journey to that point. I realized that I had built a business despite the fact that in many ways I was the bottleneck. After learning this lesson the hard way, I knew that things must change! To this end, it is very important to take the time to 'stop and smell the flowers.' In so doing, I gained insight into what characteristics provided for a successful business.

Give Back

For me, the continued success of my business relies on the support of my clients, and subsequently, of the community. As a result, giving back to the community is something that as a business owner as well as a community member, is my responsibility. It does not matter the type of donation that I provide to non-profit organizations in the community; I can and do donate my time and money, and the results and the positive impact are always encouraging and beneficial.

Taking Lesson

Many of the lessons mentioned would not have been possible without much support and expertise from many individuals and organizations. As an 8th grade student, I was taught the basic concepts of economics and business from Junior Achievement (JA), which was a vehicle for me to dream about how I could find my place among the business world. Additionally, the endless support from my parents, siblings and extended family has proven to be essential. By surrounding myself with positive, forward thinking individuals, I have been inspired to continue to grow my business. In doing so, I have developed the greatest network of mentors from different experiences each providing valid feedback for improvement. In meeting new people, I have always believed that each relationship contains differing value and potential. With this in mind, I strive to learn new skills and different perspectives from each connection I make.

Only after receiving first place in the *Minnesota Regional Global Student Entrepreneur Awards (GSEA)* competition, have I been provided access to the tools necessary to enact the aforementioned. During the fall of 2007, I was provided the opportunity to attend EO University in Las Vegas where I experienced a true renewal for my passion as an entrepreneur. At the university, I was among thousands of entrepreneurs from across the globe that had passions for many different things. After attending the most informative seminars, presentations, and speeches from some of the most successful entrepreneurs, I was again given purpose to what I do. I was provided countless skills that, if I had not attended, I would have been forced to learn them the hard way or not at all.

In November 2007, I joined over 40 young entrepreneurs like myself, from across the globe, to compete for the Global Student Entrepreneur Award. While I did not return a winner in that competition, I knew that the experiences and connections going forward would take my small retail store to the next level. Soon after, I joined the EO Chicago chapter and became a participant in the new EO Accelerator program. Through this program, I have been able to partake in quarterly learning events that have provided me access to the best resources and applicable skills in the entrepreneurial world! Today, the idea of seeking help from people smarter and more experienced than I am is very assuring. From learning that I need to work on my business and not in it, to learning to take a look from 30,000 feet, the rewards have been incalculable! Now, I travel each month to meet other entrepreneurs from the Chicago area for our accountability sessions to encourage and network for continued success.

Stop dreaming and start DOING!

As a dreamer, as an aspiring, or even as a successful entrepreneur, you have the power to create something out of nothing, to change your life and to change the world around you. The time for change is now. Have the courage to believe in yourself and in your abilities.

However, do not listen only to me, Dr. Seuss said it best, "You have brains in your head. You have feet in your shoes. You can steer yourself in any direction you choose." Here's my story, what is yours?